the naptime chef

the naptime chef

fitting great food into family life

kelsey banfield

RUNNING PRESS

PHILADELPHIA · LONDON

Copyright © 2011 by Kelsey Banfield
Photography © 2011 by Steve Legato
Published by Running Press,
A Member of the Perseus Books Group

Books published by Running Press are available at special
discounts for bulk purchases in the United States by
corporations, institutions, and other organizations. For more
information, please contact the Special Markets Department
at the Perseus Books Group, 2300 Chestnut Street, Suite 200,
Philadelphia, PA 19103, or call (800) 810-4145, ext. 5000,
or e-mail special.markets@perseusbooks.com.

ISBN 978-0-7624-4212-6
Library of Congress Control Number: 2011930505
E-book ISBN 978-0-7624-4492-2

9 8 7 6 5 4 3 2 1
Digit on the right indicates the number of this printing

Cover and interior design by Corinda Cook
Edited by Kristen Green Wiewora
Typography: Archer and Helvetica Neue

Photography by Steve Legato
Lineart food illustrations by Thomas Grillo
Food Styling by Katrina Tekavec
Food Styling Assistants. Sheila Magendantz and Kirsten Tyson
Food Styling Intern: Gigi Clark
Photo Styling by Mariellen Melker
Photo Styling Assistant: Marcy Miksic
Special thanks:
    Sur la Table, King of Prussia, PA
    Crate & Barrel, King of Prussia, PA
    Scarlett Alley, Philadelphia, PA
    Manor Home, Philadelphia, PA
    Fante's, Philadelphia, PA

Running Press Book Publishers
2300 Chestnut Street
Philadelphia, PA 19103-4371

Visit us on the web!
www.runningpresscooks.com

dedication

To Daphne and Duncan, my favorite dining companions, for their warmth, love, and appetites.

table of contents

acknowledgments

My deepest thanks to the following people:

My agent Jenni Ferrari-Adler, who believed in this project from the very start and was an endless source of advice and encouragement.

The talented team at Running Press led by my editor, Kristen Green Wiewora, who provided indispensable feedback and editing as I worked through my first manuscript.

The brilliant Steve Legato, Katrina Tekavec, and Mariellen Melker, who photographed and styled the images seen here.

Corinda Cook, who beautifully designed this entire volume.

I am so grateful to have met Adelaide Mueller, recipe tester extraordinaire, when I began this project. She carefully worked her way through every recipe in this book to ensure it was ready for print. Her professionalism and expertise were integral in producing the food on these pages.

A blogger is nothing without readers. So, thank you, dear readers—both the ones I know, and those I have yet to meet—for visiting my site every day and rooting me on.

For being my confidantes, mentors, and cheerleaders: Nicole Garwood, Wendy Littlefield, Barbara McLaughlin, Katie Rothschild, Ellen Williams, Callie Wright, and Kristina Yarrow.

It is nearly impossible to thank all of my friends in Cooperstown, New York, individually so I will just thank my hometown as a whole. I am so blessed to have grown up in such a tightly knit community to which I return time and time again. A huge thank you to everyone, especially to Mom's knitting group for testing recipes, and for their endless words of wisdom and support.

This book is all about how I feed my family, and without them I would be lost. Thank you to Patricia and Geoffrey Banfield for welcoming me into their family and making me feel right at home at their impeccably decorated table. To my parents, Roger and Carla MacMillan, for teaching me that food equals love and should always be shared with family and friends. Growing up with two parents who loved to feed and nourish their family clearly rubbed off on me. To my brother, Will, for being an impossibly hip uncle to Daphne, for teaching me about Google Docs and then using it to share his incredible collection of grilling recipes.

Thanks to Duncan, for his role as chief taste tester, for being my rock, and for taking Daphne to the playground whenever I needed to write. And, finally, a hug and kiss for Daphne, the world's sweetest baby and happiest napper. I love you to bits and chocolate chips.

introduction

about the naptime chef

The Naptime Chef is the ultimate kitchen companion for parents who love to cook and eat great food. When a baby arrives, whole hours of the day just seem to evaporate. There's less time for ingredient shopping and making complicated recipes, and less time to spend flipping through cookbooks and magazines in search of ideas and inspiration. With a young child in the house there are no more uninterrupted evening hours to leisurely prepare meals. And so parents must adapt their cooking styles to be more efficient and straightforward.

All too often, as new parents seek to modify their approach to cooking, they are told to adopt the mindset that cooking is a now a daily responsibility—a chore—and feeding their family is a problem that needs to be solved. Before children, cooking was fun! It's as if the arrival of a baby means that they ought to give up any hope of enjoying the pleasures of cooking and nourishing their families. But, what if parents actually enjoy cooking and baking? What if they are, in fact, "foodies" and love to spend time in the kitchen creating and eating delicious food with their families? How can they learn to make tasty, satisfying meals during a typically busy day?

When my daughter, Daphne, was born in 2007, I quickly realized that her naptime was my free time to get things done, and this included cooking. If I wanted to enjoy my passion for creating and enjoying great food, I had to use that window of time to my advantage. Having a child also meant I had to develop some new skills and techniques in order to meet the daily needs of a hungry family no matter how much, or how little, time I had available. I reinvented my cooking style and became The Naptime Chef.

becoming the naptime chef

The first few weeks after Daphne was born were a blur. Getting dressed each day felt like a major accomplishment, and take-out was our main source of nourishment. But after a month or two we fell into a daily rhythm, and I got excited to return to the kitchen. It was time to dust off my favorite recipes and flip through the growing stack of food magazines on my nightstand. Except instead of jumping right back into the swing of things I found myself putting together meals with only moderate success, hampered by an unfamiliar clumsiness. Everything felt strange and uncomfortable as I sliced and diced (more often than not, with an upset baby on my hip). I didn't know to plan or prep anything ahead of time. I'd always loved getting home from work and pouring myself a glass of wine, taking my time with dinner. Post-baby, when dinner hour arrived I was so tired I scrapped any plans for cooking. Evening was also Daphne's fussiest time—and soon became mine too! Despite my best efforts, she was rarely content enough to let me get things done, making it my least productive time of day.

For weeks I couldn't figure out how to get anything more than microwaved meals on the table. It was frustrating, but I was determined to produce at least one delicious meal a day and reestablish my place at the helm of our kitchen. I resorted to tossing plush and noisy toys at Daphne in an attempt to placate her, but she would have none of it and my visions of yummy homemade meals faded with every cry.

After several disastrous attempts to recreate our favorite dishes, including a particularly poor version of Creamy Artichoke Lasagna, which we promptly threw out in favor of take-out, I put my foot down. I was tired of eating so-so meals, and I swore I would find a way to cook: not just cook, but cook *well*, and not just well on occasion, but well on a daily basis.

Making my favorite Creamy Artichoke Lasagna required an uninterrupted forty-five minutes that I no longer had in the evening. I began to wonder: could I prepare parts of it during the day to make assembly easier at dinner hour? Which other of my favorite recipes could I streamline? I became focused on preparing food efficiently while still maintaining quality and taste. The recipes I wanted to make weren't complicated or difficult: it was food that we had always loved, and still loved even as parents. We just had to get creative.

One day, while Daphne was napping, I put in a load of laundry and chopped some of the vegetables that were about to overstay their welcome in the crisper drawer. In fifteen minutes I had a bowl of prepped vegetables and a load of laundry ready for the dryer. Almost without thinking, I placed half the vegetables in my stockpot with some stock and seasonings, set it to simmer, and had a delicious minestrone soup on my hands in no time at all. The rest of the vegetables I bagged up and placed in the fridge to toss with pasta the following evening. As I contentedly stirred my soup, I realized that cooking during naptime was the answer! With a little planning I'd be able to prepare an entire main course, or at least assemble the ingredients for one, while Daphne napped. Then, in the evening all I had to do was add heat or assemble the dishes in their final form, like tossing together the salad or boiling fresh pasta. These steps took minutes, not hours, making the hours before dinner much more pleasant since I could look forward to great food without the chaos of trying to cook from scratch.

Emboldened by this realization, I decided to roast a chicken. I seasoned it during naptime and left it in the fridge for a few hours before cooking it. Success! In fact, the chicken was so moist and flavorful I now recommend that everyone prepare chicken in advance and allow it to rest a few hours before roasting whenever possible.

What a thrill and a relief! By setting aside some time in the kitchen while Daphne napped, I enjoyed cooking and eating great food again.

Of course, I didn't cook for her entire naptime each and every day, but with some simple planning I had all the time I needed to create delicious meals that nourished my family.

When I already had leftovers from the previous night, or we'd made dinner plans, I used naptime to bake treats to serve at playgroup, stock the freezer with homemade meatballs or pesto, make fruit jams from scratch, or tackle breakfast foods like large batches of homemade granola, jars of pancake mix, and make-ahead French toast. Every time I thought of a new recipe to try I always made sure that I could prepare the whole thing, or at least parts of it, during naptime.

the blog

Once I was in the rhythm of cooking primarily during naptimes I began wondering how I could parlay my ideas into a fun and satisfying project. Since I'd been sharing my Naptime Chef stories with friends for almost a year, it seemed like writing them down along with my recipes and stories would be a great place to start. So, in January 2009 I started my blog, The Naptime Chef (www.thenaptimechef.com), about how I fit great food into our family life.

I had come up with the name during one of our weekly playgroups. At this gathering a few mothers were commiserating about the lousy meals they'd been serving. They confessed to relying heavily on frozen meals, cold cereal, and take-out. I explained my idea of cooking during naptime and how it enabled me to produce dishes like homemade Italian-style meatloaf on a daily basis. "It's easy," I told them, "I use naptime to relax and enjoy my time in the kitchen. I am The Naptime Chef!" The name stuck from the moment I said it.

The blog is my personal food diary, where I share the real-life scenarios that frame our daily meals. In it I blend the voice of the parent and the foodie. I don't make food just to have something on the table, I write about food I *love* to cook and eat in order to demonstrate how parents can do the

same in their own kitchens. I also write about strategies for stocking the pantry and freezer, and the dishes I make for family entertaining, bake sales, and taking to new parents. I cook mostly during Daphne's afternoon naptime or after her bedtime, and leave the final assembly until right before we want to eat.

The Naptime Chef acknowledges that having a child forces us to change our cooking style, but it doesn't need to change what we make. By cooking during your baby's naptime, you can enjoy leisurely time in the kitchen to prepare tasty family food. It isn't about offering formulaic solutions to dinnertime or implying that cooking is for suffering through. This book reflects the idea that parents can still experience the pleasures of cooking and eating great food each and every day.

how you can be a naptime chef

Being a naptime chef is about picking recipes that work with your day, your week, and your life, and fitting them into your schedule. You certainly don't have to cook through entire naptimes, seven days a week! When you have lots of time and energy, enjoy more involved recipes. When you are totally exhausted, or need time for chores, whip up something simple and quick. (Look for the Naptime Stopwatches throughout the book: they'll tell you at a glance how much prep time you need to set aside.) If you have no time to cook, take advantage of the frozen foods you keep stocked in the freezer. No matter what you choose, the food you make can be always be delicious and satisfying.

People always ask me what I will do when Daphne gives up naps. I tell them that I will cook when she is at school, at soccer practice, or generally occupied with some other activity. Being a naptime chef starts when the babies are napping, but continues until they are grown and out of the house. The 5 o'clock pm witching hour you experience with infants transforms into bus pick-up time or dreaded homework hour. The early evening busy period never ends. If there is free time earlier in the day when the

kids are at school, use it to cook just like you did when the babies were napping. Dinner will be on the table with minimal fuss and everyone can slow down for a least a few minutes to enjoy a wholesome, nourishing meal in the midst of the daily grind.

If you are a working parent, be a bedtime chef and prepare dinner ahead for the next day. Many of the dishes in the cookbook can be prepared up to a day or more ahead of time before being eaten. There are also plenty of recipes for stocking the freezer and pantry that can help make cooking a delicious dinner after work a breeze. Happiness in the kitchen is within your grasp. A small amount of planning about when and what you want to cook makes the all the difference.

The point is, the time is there. Find where it is in your day and fit great food into your family life.

naptime chef kitchen basics

You don't have to own loads of expensive equipment to cook well. Over the years I've been gifted many wonderful kitchen tools and have bought a few things of my own, but I had it all long before Daphne was born. Here are a few of the things I think are essential for any naptime chef kitchen. Of course, use what you wish and substitute as necessary based on your space and budget.

tools & utensils

measuring cups and spoons: These often double as toys in my house so buy sets that are durable and dishwasher-friendly. If they go missing, try looking in the bathtub or sandbox.

openers: A handheld can opener is key. A wine opener/bottle opener is also essential, especially at the end of a long day. Instead of buying complicated lever wine openers buy basic corkscrews that are more durable and cheaper to replace.

oven mitts: A set of two silicone oven mitts has saved my fingers from

being permanently burned. They also can be dressed up to make puppets in a pinch on a rainy day.

over-the-sink colander: A sturdy colander is essential when draining a full pot of pasta. An over-the-sink version is also excellent for sweating eggplant, cleaning leeks, and rinsing small toys.

peeler: Invest in a good peeler that is sharp and easy to grip. These can handle the harder vegetables like squash and eggplant and enable you to peel apples and carrots in record-breaking time when the snack time countdown is on.

spatulas: A set of good silicone spatulas (one large, one medium) can be used for everything from stirring soups and sauces to spreading cake batter. Their soft ends are excellent for teething babies. Flexible metal spatulas are a must for flipping pancakes, eggs, or any delicate foods, and a sturdy metal spatula is key for serving heavy baked pastas out of bakers. An offset spatula is the best for icing cakes.

whisks: A set of whisks (one large, one small) can be used for everything from whisking dressings and eggs to making whipped cream by hand. A whisk is also a great kitchen tool for kids learning to mix ingredients.

thermometers: The candy thermometer is the best way to determine the temperature of jams and the meat thermometer is the best way to determine the internal temperature of meats and roasts.

long-handled heatproof tongs: Tongs are ideal for flipping chicken cutlets, retrieving long strands of pasta from the pot and adjusting ingredients cooking in hot oil. Other handy uses include retrieving toys from underneath the furniture where your hand can't reach.

grater/zester: A microplane zester and box grater are key in the kitchen. The box grater is essential for cheeses and vegetables. The zester can be used for everything from chocolate and citrus to nutmeg and garlic.

wooden spoons: A long-handled wooden spoon is key for protecting your arms when stirring hot soups and grains like polenta or risotto. They also make perfect drumsticks for overturned pots.

knives: The serrated knife (bread knife) is the best way to cut bread and tomatoes. One good chef's knife is key to cutting meats, pastas, and brownies. Be sure to sharpen it regularly to avoid risk of injury. I find that buying inexpensive paring knives is the best way to go. Like the chef's knife, a paring knife should be razor-sharp to prevent slippage. If you

can't cut through a tomato, sharpen the knife immediately or throw it out and start over. Having one or two extra paring knives on hand means you will always be well-equipped.

countertop

food processor: A good food processor can be costly, but will last a lifetime when maintained properly. It can be used for everything from chopping vegetables to making soups and pie crusts.

stand mixer or hand mixer: I use a stand mixer, but a hand mixer works just as well for most recipes.

blender or hand-blender: The best way to get a soup silky-smooth is with a blender or with a hand (or immersion) blender. These are also excellent for makings smoothies and pureeing any of your meals to make baby food.

nesting bowls: Bowls of various sizes can be used for everything from mixing batters to setting out a mise en place before cooking. Buy a set that is dishwasher-friendly and very durable. It is important that one or more of them is heatproof so that it can be made into a double boiler.

cutting board/butcher block: A non-slip cutting board is key for cooking. I recommend buying one that is lightweight and easily maneuvered so that chopped foods can be deposited straight into pots and pans. Be sure to clean and maintain your cutting board with hot water and soap to avoid any bacteria build-up.

stovetop

4-quart saucepan with lid: This is the pot I use the most. In fact, there is hardly anything I haven't used it for yet. Buy one with a tight-fitting lid so that it can be used for steaming rice and vegetables as well as boiling pasta. This also the best pan to use as the base for a double boiler.

3-quart sauté pan: This is my second most-used pan. I even bought a splatter screen to go over the top: it is essential when I am cooking with oil over high heat.

8-inch nonstick skillet: Make sure any skillet you buy has an ovenproof handle. This makes it so easy to bake frittatas or keep food warm.

10-inch nonstick skillet: A large skillet is useful for making pancakes or sautéing large batches of chicken at once.

dutch ovens: These are more expensive pieces but are worth the investment. A 7-quart Dutch oven is ideal for slow braises, soups, and jams. The 2¾-quart Dutch oven is perfect for baking no-knead bread.

oven

These are the basic baking pans I recommend owning:

- 13 x 9 baking dish
- 18 x 13 jelly roll pan (rimmed baking sheet)
- 16 x 14 baking sheet (at least 2)
- 9 x 9 baking dish
- 9 x 5 loaf pan
- 12-cup muffin tin
- 9-inch pie plate
- 9-inch springform pan
- 9-inch tart pan with removable bottom
- 9-inch round cake pans (at least 2)
- Large roasting pan with rack

ingredients

flour: When I refer to flour in these pages, I mean unbleached all-purpose flour.

eggs: All of the eggs in this book are large eggs.

milk: Unless otherwise noted, the milk is whole.

butter: I use unsalted butter throughout this book, unless otherwise noted.

morning foods

strawberries & cream overnight french toast

It's a simple luxury to wake up to breakfast ready to go. I assemble this at night after Daphne is asleep and let it chill in the fridge. In the morning, I pop it in the oven, set the timer, and brew some coffee. By the time everyone is awake and at the table, the timer dings and a hot, hearty breakfast is ready! With a healthy drizzle of warm maple syrup and a dollop of whipped cream, a slice of this sweet berry custard it is just the thing to get our day started.

 naptime
stopwatch

20 minutes prep time
50 minutes bake time

makes 8 to 10 servings

Unsalted butter, as needed

1 loaf day-old challah bread

2 cups heavy whipping cream

2 cups whole milk

8 large eggs

1 teaspoon vanilla extract

5 teaspoons granulated sugar

1 teaspoon ground cinnamon

½ teaspoon kosher salt

1 pint fresh strawberries, hulled and sliced (or substitute frozen, about 1½ cups)

1 cup maple syrup, warmed

1. Butter a 13 x 9-inch baking dish, paying special attention to the corners and bottom.

2. Cut the challah into 1-inch-thick slices and arrange them in the baking dish so that they are overlapping and fit together snugly.

3. In a large bowl, whisk together the cream, milk, eggs, vanilla, sugar, cinnamon, and salt until blended.

4. Pour the egg mixture over the bread, drizzling it back and forth across the dish so the bread is evenly coated. Using your fingers, press the bread down to immerse it in the egg mixture. It is fine if it springs back up after a minute or so, so long as it is saturated.

5. Cover the baking dish with plastic wrap and place it in the refrigerator for at least 4 hours, or overnight.

6. Preheat the oven to 350°F.

7. Remove the plastic wrap from the baking dish. Tuck three-quarters of the sliced strawberries between the bread slices and scatter the remaining berries evenly on top. Place the baking dish on a cookie sheet and bake for 45 to 50 minutes, or until the top is lightly browned, the bread has absorbed all of the liquid, and the custard is puffed up. Remove from the oven and cool for 5 minutes before slicing and serving with a drizzle of maple syrup.

serving ideas: This is a terrific dish for serving overnight guests or at a buffet brunch. The hostess can make it ahead of time and the only thing to be done the day of the party is to bake it. To make it really decadent, serve it with whipped cream or a scoop of ice cream: then it truly becomes dessert for breakfast. And nobody ever complains about that!

variation ideas: This is a great recipe for any time of year and works well with blueberries or raspberries (or both!) if you don't have strawberries on hand.

orange cinnamon chip scones

Scones are one of the best make-ahead breakfasts around. The dough is incredibly simple to make in advance whenever you have a spare moment and lasts for a few days in the refrigerator before baking. Best of all, everyone raves about your mad baking skills when you serve them fresh from the oven.

naptime stopwatch

10 minutes prep time
25 minutes bake time

makes 8 scones

2 cups all-purpose flour, plus more for tossing the chips

⅓ cup granulated sugar

½ teaspoon baking soda

1 teaspoon baking powder

1 tablespoon freshly grated orange zest (about 1 medium orange)

6 tablespoons chilled butter, cut into small pieces

¾ cup cinnamon chips

1 large egg yolk

¾ cup heavy cream

1 teaspoon vanilla extract

3 tablespoons raw sugar

1. Preheat the oven to 400°F. Line a baking sheet with parchment paper or a silicone liner.

2. Sift the flour, sugar, baking soda, and baking powder together into a bowl. Add the orange zest and use your fingertips to rub it with some of the sugar to release and enhance the orange flavor.

3. Add the chilled butter pieces to the dry ingredients and work them in with your hands or a pastry blender until the mixture resembles small peas. Toss the cinnamon chips with a pinch of flour and add them to the butter mixture.

4. In a separate bowl, whisk together the egg yolk, heavy cream, and vanilla. Pour the cream mixture into the butter mixture in a steady stream, stirring continuously until everything is incorporated and a sticky dough forms. Reserve the bowl that contained the yolk, cream, and extract.

5. Remove the dough from the bowl and place it on a lightly floured work surface. Use the heel of your hand to press the dough into a circle that is 1-inch thick, then cut the dough into 8 even-sized wedges and place them on the prepared baking sheet. Use a pastry brush to lift up the remaining yolk, cream, and vanilla extract from the reserved bowl and brush a thin layer of the cream mixture on the top of each scone, followed by a sprinkle of the raw sugar.

6. Bake the scones for about 25 to 28 minutes, or until the edges are golden brown.

make-ahead tips: The prepared dough can be pressed into the 1-inch-thick circle, wrapped tightly in plastic wrap and stored it in the refrigerator for up to 3 days before baking. Or, the dough can be wrapped in a double layer of plastic wrap and an outer layer of aluminum foil and frozen for up to 3 months. Bring the dough to room temperature before baking.

variation ideas: Mini chocolate chips, chocolate chunks, or dried cherries all taste great in lieu of cinnamon chips. Mix it up and have fun!

homemade malted pancake mix

A well-stocked pantry is the key to my sanity. Once a month, I mix together a dry pancake mix and store it in a basic quart jar. Having this on hand means I never have to worry about what to make for breakfast if nothing has been prepared the night before. The key to these delicious pancakes is malted milk powder. My brother gave me the idea after he coerced the chef at the hotel he worked at one summer into sharing the secret ingredient for his signature pancake recipe. Malt elevates the flavor of this ordinary breakfast staple, giving the pancakes nutty undertones and a smooth creamy finish.

naptime stopwatch

5 minutes prep time

makes 5 cups

4 cups unbleached all-purpose flour

1 cup malted milk powder

1 teaspoon ground cinnamon

3 tablespoons baking powder

2 teaspoons baking soda

2 tablespoons granulated sugar

2 teaspoons kosher salt

Combine all the ingredients in a bowl and stir with a whisk until completely combined. Store in an airtight container for up to 6 months.

To cook, see page 31.

make-ahead tips: Baking powder doesn't stay good forever, so it is wise to use the pancake mix within 6 months of making it. Store it in an airtight jar to maintain freshness. For a fun home-made gift, wrap a ribbon around the lid and give it to friends with a card containing cooking instructions.

creamy malted pancakes

 naptime
stopwatch

10 minutes cook time

makes 7 to 8
five-inch pancakes

1 large egg

1 cup whole milk

1 cup Homemade Malted
Pancake Mix (page 29)

1 tablespoon unsalted butter,
plus more as needed

1. Preheat the oven to 200°F.

2. Whisk together the egg and milk in a large bowl. Add the dry pancake mix and whisk until the batter is smooth and creamy.

3. Heat the butter in a large skillet over medium heat. Swirl the pan gently so that the butter covers the entire bottom.

4. Ladle ⅓ cup portions of the batter into the skillet so that they are close together, but not touching, and cook the pancakes until bubbles start to show on the surface. Using a small, flexible spatula, flip the pancakes and cook them on the other side until lightly golden brown.

5. Repeat to make additional batches, adding more butter to the pan as needed. Hold the freshly cooked pancakes in the warm oven, wrapped in a kitchen towel or in aluminum foil, until ready to serve.

serving ideas: Pancakes are the ideal canvas for all sorts of flavors and textures. Try topping them with fresh seasonal berries, yogurt, whipped cream, or a soft cheese. Our favorite topping is warm syrup and toasted chopped pecans.

ultimate buttermilk coffee cake bars

I first tasted these creamy breakfast cake bars when my neighbor, Sarah Turner, served them at a casual holiday brunch. I immediately fell for the contrast of the fine, crunchy topping and tender crumb. Turns out she'd inherited the recipe from her grandmother-in-law, a baker of reputation in her small town in Wisconsin. Accustomed to entertaining, this woman wrote the coffee cake recipe to serve a crowd, baking it in a sheet pan instead of the more traditional tube pan. This way, the cake can be cut into easy-to-handle bars.

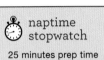

naptime stopwatch

25 minutes prep time
30 minutes bake time

makes 20 bars

1 cup (2 sticks) plus 6 table-spoons unsalted butter, at room temperature, divided, plus more as needed for the pan

1 ⅓ cups granulated sugar, divided

1 ⅓ cups packed dark brown sugar, divided

3 ⅔ cups plus 3 tablespoons all-purpose flour, divided, plus more as needed for the pan

¼ teaspoon kosher salt

1 teaspoon baking soda

2 large eggs, at room temperature

1 cup cultured buttermilk

3 teaspoons vanilla extract

½ cup finely chopped pecans (optional)

1. Preheat the oven to 350°F. Butter and flour an 18 x 13-inch jelly roll pan or cookie sheet with 1-inch-high sides and set aside.

2. Set 3 mixing bowls on your countertop, 1 large and 2 small. In the large mixing bowl, combine 2 sticks of butter, 1 cup of granulated sugar, 1 cup of brown sugar, and 3 cups plus 3 tablespoons of flour. Blend these ingredients together with a wooden spoon until large pebbles form. Add the salt and baking soda and mix again.

2. In one small bowl, lightly beat the eggs with the buttermilk and vanilla until completely combined; pour the mixture into the dry ingredients. Using a wooden spoon, mix until the batter is smooth and everything is evenly incorporated.

3. In the second small bowl, add the remaining ⅓ cup granulated sugar, ⅓ cup brown sugar, 6 tablespoons butter, and ⅔ cups flour. Blend these together with your fingers until the mixture is very fine, almost like coarse sand. This takes a little bit of time; it works best when you rub the ingredients between your thumbs and forefingers. Stir in the finely chopped pecans and set aside.

4. Pour the batter from the large bowl into the prepared baking pan and smooth the top with a rubber spatula. Sprinkle the sugar-pecan mixture evenly over the top of the batter, covering the batter right to the edge of the pan.

5. Bake the cake for 25 to 30 minutes, or until the cake has risen slightly and the center is set. It should spring back when lightly touched in the middle. Allow the cake to cool for about 10 minutes, cut into 3-inch squares, and serve.

make-ahead tips: This moist cake will keep covered for 1 to 2 days. To prevent it from drying out, don't cut the bars until just before serving.

variation ideas: The pecans can be omitted if necessary. Or, if pecans aren't available, substitute chopped walnuts.

caramel-stuffed cinnamon muffins

How do you improve upon the perfect fall breakfast muffin? By adding caramel, of course! This bit of wisdom did not come from me, but from my friend's six-year-old son. The caramel settles toward the bottom of the muffins as they bake and is a sweet surprise with each bite. I love serving these cake-like muffins at fall brunches; their warm cinnamon-orange flavor pairs perfectly with mulled cider and the autumnal colors of the season.

 naptime stopwatch

15 minutes prep time
15 minutes bake time

makes 12 muffins

muffins

1½ cups all-purpose flour

¾ cup granulated sugar

2 teaspoons baking powder

½ teaspoon salt

1 teaspoon freshly grated orange zest

½ teaspoon freshly grated nutmeg

1 teaspoon ground cinnamon

½ cup whole milk

1 large egg, lightly beaten

4 ounces (1 stick) unsalted butter, melted, cooled, and divided

12 soft caramels, unwrapped

topping

2 tablespoons granulated sugar

2 tablespoons ground cinnamon

1. Preheat the oven to 375°F. Butter a 12-cup muffin pan or line the cups with paper liners and set aside.

2. In a small bowl, mix the flour, sugar, baking powder, salt, orange zest, nutmeg, and cinnamon.

3. In a large bowl, whisk together the milk, egg, and all but 2 tablespoons of the melted butter until completely combined.

4. Gently pour the flour mixture into the egg mixture, stirring with a wooden spoon until everything is just incorporated and the flour is no longer visible.

5. Spoon the batter into the muffin cups until they are each one-third full. Place a caramel in the center of each muffin. Cover the caramel with the remaining batter until each muffin cup is two-thirds full.

6. Bake the muffins for 15 to 17 minutes, or until the tops are lightly browned and spring back when touched, rotating the pan halfway through baking. Remove the muffins from the pan, place them on a wire rack and allow them to cool for 10 minutes, or until they are comfortable to hold in your hand.

7. In a small bowl, combine the cinnamon and sugar for the topping. Brush each muffin 2 to 3 times with the remaining 2 tablespoons of melted butter and lightly dip the top of each muffin in the cinnamon-sugar mixture. Serve warm.

make-ahead tips: This batter can be made up to a day ahead of baking time. To store the batter, place it in a small bowl in the refrigerator covered with plastic wrap pressed directly onto the surface of the batter. Bring the batter to room temperature before proceeding with Step 5. Alternatively, these muffins can be baked a day ahead and stored in an airtight container. Wait to add the cinnamon-sugar topping until right before serving. Warm them in the oven or microwave, then add the topping as instructed in Step 7.

old-fashioned blueberry muffins

My friend Mary learned to make these flakey biscuit-like muffins from her neighbor, Ethel Wolf, growing up in Pennsylvania. Mary, in turn, made them for her own children and has passed down the recipe to her grandchildren, as well. I love making these at home. They are much lighter than muffins from the coffee shop, and a much more manageable size, too.

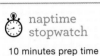

naptime stopwatch

10 minutes prep time
15 minutes bake time

makes 14 to 15 muffins

2 cups all-purpose flour

¼ cup plus 2 tablespoons granulated sugar

½ teaspoon salt

4 teaspoons baking powder

Zest from 1 medium lemon

4 ounces (1 stick) unsalted butter, chilled

1 large egg

¾ cup whole milk

1½ cups fresh blueberries, rinsed and patted dry

1. Preheat the oven to 425°F. Butter a 12-cup muffin pan or line the cups with paper liners and set aside.

2. In a large bowl, mix the flour, sugar, salt, baking powder, and zest. Cut the butter into small cubes and pinch it into the dry ingredients with your hands or with a pastry cutter. This takes a few minutes to do. The batter will look like a bowl of small buttery pebbles once the butter and dry ingredients are properly incorporated.

3. In a separate bowl, lightly whisk together the egg and milk. Pour the egg mixture into the dry ingredients and stir with a wooden spoon until fully combined. The mixture will look a little lumpy and gluey.

4. Carefully stir the blueberries into the batter with a rubber spatula so as not to crush them, until just combined. Spoon the batter into each muffin cup until it is three-quarters full.

5. Bake the muffins for 15 to 17 minutes, or until the tops are golden and spring back when touched, rotating the pan halfway through baking.

make-ahead tips: This batter keeps well in the refrigerator overnight if you want to serve fresh-baked muffins in the morning. Cover the bowl with plastic wrap pressed directly onto the batter. Alternatively, bake the muffins the day before, store them in an airtight container, and warm them in the oven or microwave prior to serving.

variation ideas: Raspberries, wine berries, or cranberries are all excellent substitutes if blueberries aren't available.

holiday nut rolls

My friend Terry Maulsby and her daughter Jennifer have been giving these as Christmas gifts to their friends for so many years they've become tradition. Our Christmas morning buffet wouldn't be complete without it! Terry is a mom of three and well-versed on making things ahead of time. These sweet rolls have become part of our family's holiday tradition too. Plan ahead; the dough needs to rest for 24 hours.

 **naptime stopwatch**

1 hour prep time
40 minutes bake time

makes 16 to 20 servings

dough

1 (¼ ounce) package active dry yeast

1 cup whole milk, warmed (about 110 °F)

1 tablespoon plus 1 pinch granulated sugar

4 ounces (1 stick) unsalted butter, melted and cooled

4 large eggs

1 cup evaporated milk

4 cups all-purpose flour

1 teaspoon salt

filling

Reserved 4 large egg whites (from Dough; see step 2)

1 cup granulated sugar

(continued)

1. *To make the dough:* In a large bowl, dissolve yeast in warm milk with a pinch of sugar. Gently stir the yeast into the milk with a fork to begin the dissolving process.

2. Crack the eggs and separate the egg whites from the yolks. Add the egg whites to a sealed container and store in the refrigerator until you are ready to make the filling (about 24 hours later). Beat the egg yolks in a separate bowl with a fork. Add the yolks and cooled butter to the milk and yeast, followed by the evaporated milk, flour, salt, and sugar. Mix the ingredients with a wooden spoon until just combined. The dough will be wet and sticky.

3. Divide the dough into 4 evenly sized balls and individually wrap each one tightly in plastic wrap. Place in them in the refrigerator for at least 24 hours.

4. Preheat the oven to 350°F. Line a cookie sheet with parchment paper or silicone liner and set aside.

5. *To make the filling:* In a mixer fitted with the whisk attachment beat the egg whites until light and frothy, about 1 minute. Add the sugar and vanilla and whisk for about 3 to 4 minutes, or until they hold stiff peaks. Stir in the walnuts with a wooden spoon and set aside.

6. Remove the four balls of dough from the refrigerator and place them on a generously floured surface. Roll out each ball of into a rectangle, about 12 inches in length and ⅛ inch thick. Divide the filling among the pieces of dough and spread evenly within the rectangle, leaving a 1 inch border.

7. Working carefully, pinch in both of the long sides of the dough just over the filling. Then roll the dough, starting from one of the short ends, and arrange on the baking sheets, seam-side down. The rolls should resemble logs.

8. Bake the rolls for 35 minutes, or until they are golden brown and spring back to the touch. Place on a wire rack to cool.

9. *To make the frosting:* In a mixer fitted with the paddle attachment, cream the butter and cream cheese on medium speed until completely smooth, about 2 minutes. Add the confectioners' sugar, vanilla, and milk and beat until smooth and fluffy on low-medium speed. Generously cover the tops of each roll with an even layer of frosting once they have cooled completely. Slice each roll into 4 or 5 slices and serve warm.

make-ahead tips: This project is best spread out across two nap-times. Prepare the dough the first day and proceed with the filling and frosting the next. Once frosted, these rolls will freeze beautifully. Flash-freeze the frosted rolls (uncovered for about 2 hours) first, then wrap them tightly in plastic wrap followed by a layer of aluminum foil. (This keeps the frosting from being crushed with the plastic wrap.) The rolls will stay in the freezer like this for up to 4 months.

variation ideas: For a festive look, add a few drops of green or red food coloring to the frosting before frosting the nut rolls. Or, sprinkle the frosting with a touch of cinnamon and cocoa powder to add a little spice.

1 teaspoon vanilla extract

1 pound walnuts, finely chopped

frosting

4 ounces (1 stick) unsalted butter, at room temperature

4 ounces cream cheese, at room temperature

4 cups confectioners' sugar

1 teaspoon vanilla extract

2 tablespoons whole milk

anytime vegetable pie

Cheesy quiches are a favorite of mine for weekend brunches or light suppers. I first tasted this variation at my own baby shower. The hostess, Christine, served this veggie-laden pie to a dozen of my closest friends and one very hungry pregnant lady. Thank goodness she made two: I nearly polished off half of one by myself! I received many wonderful gifts that day but I think this recipe was my favorite.

naptime stopwatch

30 minutes prep time
55 minutes bake time

makes one 9-inch pie

crust

4 ounces (1 stick) unsalted butter, chilled

1 ½ cups all-purpose flour

Pinch of kosher salt

¼ cup ice water

filling

1 teaspoon olive oil

1 red bell pepper, finely chopped

Half of 1 red onion, finely chopped

2 garlic cloves, minced

4 large eggs

1 cup half-and-half

2 cups (8 ounces) shredded Monterey Jack cheese

(continued)

1. *To make the crust:* Combine the butter, flour, salt, and ice water to a food processor and give it a few quick pulses until they become crumbly and dough begins to form. Dump the mixture from the food processor onto a lightly floured surface and gather the dough into a ball with your hands. You may need to knead it a couple of times to form it into a tight ball. (If you are not going to bake it immediately, wrap the ball of dough tightly in plastic wrap and refrigerate for 24 hours. Let the dough sit at room temperature, about 15 minutes, before rolling out.)

2. Using a lightly floured rolling pin, roll out the dough until it is 10 inches in diameter and transfer it onto a 9-inch pie plate. Press the dough into the pie plate and trim any excess with scissors. Prick the surface all around with fork tines and crimp the edge, if you'd like, to make a decorative pattern. Chill the pie crust in the plate for 1 hour in the refrigerator.

3. Preheat the oven to 375°F.

4. Fill the crust with pie weights or dried beans and bake it for 15 minutes, or until it is lightly golden. Remove pie weights or dried beans. Maintain oven temperature.

5. *To make the filling:* In a large sauté pan, heat the olive oil over medium heat until it is hot, but not smoking. Add the chopped bell pepper and onion and cook until they are soft, stirring occasionally so they don't burn. Add the garlic and cook for another minute, or until it is fragrant.

6. When the vegetables are cooked through, remove the pan from the heat and allow it to cool for 5 minutes.

7. In a large bowl, whisk together the eggs, half-and-half, and both cheeses. Pour the cooled vegetables into the egg mixture and add the salt and basil. Stir the filling a few times to combine.

8. Pour the egg mixture into the prepared crust and gently arrange 4 or 5 of the tomato slices decoratively on top.

9. Bake the pie for about 55 to 60 minutes, or until the top is set and no longer wiggles in the center when the pan is shaken. It will be lightly browned and bubbly on top. Allow to cool out of the oven for 10 minutes. Cut into slices and serve warm.

⅓ cup (1 ½ ounces) freshly grated Parmesan cheese

1 teaspoon kosher salt

1 tablespoon coarsely chopped fresh basil

1 tomato, sliced into ¼-inch thick slices

make-ahead tips: The crust can be baked up to 6 hours before adding the filling. I often bake it in the morning or during naptime before adding the filling for dinner. For brunches, bake the crust the night before, then make the filling in the morning. To store the baked crust, wrap it in a layer of plastic wrap and refrigerate for up to 24 hours before using. It can be frozen in a double layer of plastic wrap and an outer layer of aluminum foil for up to 3 months.

variation ideas: You can use an endless variety of veggies in this dish. The main rule of thumb is to use about 1 cup of cooked vegetables per pie, in addition to the onion and garlic. I have substituted green bell peppers, mushrooms, broccoli, caramelized onions, and wilted spinach for the red bell pepper. Each addition has been a hit! For some extra decadence, dot the top of the pie with tangy goat cheese right before baking.

mixed-berry cream cheese

I always come home from our summer berry picking excursions with more fresh fruit than I know what to do with. I started making this spread as a way to use up some berries and add new flavor to our favorite bagel breakfast. With one simple step the sweet berries and tangy cheese come together to form a fruity spread that we all love.

naptime stopwatch

10 minutes prep time

makes about 3 cups

16 ounces (two 8-ounce packages) plain cream cheese, at room temperature

½ cup fresh strawberries, washed, hulled, and quartered

½ cup fresh blueberries, washed and dried

½ cup fresh raspberries, washed and dried

2 teaspoons honey

½ teaspoon ground cinnamon

Combine all ingredients in a food processor fitted with a blade. Pulse several times until the berries are evenly incorporated.

make-ahead tips: This cream cheese will keep in a sealed container in the refrigerator for up to a week. It can also be made ahead and frozen in a tightly sealed container for up to 3 months.

serving ideas: This tangy fruit spread is heaven on bagels, English muffins, and thick-cut toast. It also makes a great afternoon snack spread on a crispy whole wheat cracker.

variation ideas: Blackberries, wine berries, or huckleberries would also taste wonderful mixed with cream cheese. Use what is freshest and available near you.

cranberry spice granola

This granola is a mainstay in my pantry. I munch on it all day long, sometimes skipping lunch because I eat so much at breakfast. Whenever the jar gets low I rush to make another batch during naptime. God forbid I'm without it for even a day! Packaged in a jar with a pretty bow, this makes an excellent gift.

 **naptime stopwatch**

10 minutes prep time
20 minutes bake time

makes about 6 cups

⅓ cup plus 1 teaspoon vegetable oil, divided

3 cups old-fashioned oats (not quick-cooking)

1 cup sweetened shredded coconut

1 cup (4 ounces) pecans, coarsely chopped

1 teaspoon fine sea salt

1 teaspoon ground cinnamon

¼ teaspoon ground nutmeg

¼ teaspoon ground ginger

1 teaspoon vanilla extract

½ cup pure Grade A maple syrup

¼ cup apple cider or apple juice

1 cup dried cranberries

1. Preheat the oven to 350°F. Rub the bottom and sides of an 18 x 13-inch rimmed baking sheet with 1 teaspoon of vegetable oil and set aside.

2. In a large mixing bowl, combine the oats, coconut, pecans, salt, cinnamon, nutmeg, and ginger. Stir these together with a wooden spoon so the oats and spices are evenly incorporated. In a separate bowl, whisk together the remaining ⅓ cup oil, vanilla extract, maple syrup, and apple cider, and pour it evenly over the oat mixture. Stir the oats until they are coated with the liquids, working carefully so as not to crush them. The mixture will be sticky once everything is mixed together.

3. Spread the oat mixture on the prepared baking sheet in an even layer and bake it for 10 minutes without disturbing. Remove the baking sheet from the oven and place it on the countertop. Stir the granola with a long-handled wooden spoon, turning everything over so it will toast evenly. Return the pan to the oven and bake for an additional 10 to 12 minutes, or until it is golden brown and fragrant. Remove the pan from the oven and immediately add the dried cranberries to the mixture, stirring them in lightly with a wooden spoon.

4. Allow the granola to cool on the counter for an hour or so. It will crisp and harden as it cools. Store the granola in a cool dry place, preferably in a jar with a tight-fitting lid.

serving ideas: Granola is perhaps the most versatile of breakfast foods. Eat it with milk, sprinkled over yogurt or pancakes, or dry out of the bowl. Pack it in baggies for the kids to take to school. It's a great snack to keep in your purse, too!

variation ideas: Granola can be adapted to suit nearly every taste. For a tropical flavor, substitute dried pineapple slices and pineapple juice for the cranberries and apple cider. If you don't have pecans on hand, almonds or walnuts are excellent alternatives.

small bites and salads

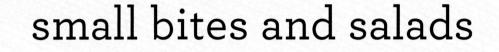

mascarpone-stuffed strawberries

These are like inside-out strawberry cheesecakes. Ripe red berries stuffed with a touch of mascarpone, they are the perfect summer snack for kids and adults alike. For a festive Fourth of July flair, top each with a blueberry!

naptime stopwatch

30 minutes prep time

makes 20 to 25
stuffed strawberries

1 quart fresh medium-
to-large strawberries

1 ¼ cups (10 ounces)
mascarpone cheese,
at room temperature

3 tablespoons confectioners'
sugar

1 teaspoon vanilla extract

1 teaspoon ground cinnamon
(optional)

1. Using a small sharp knife, carefully hull each berry and slice it in half. Place the strawberry halves, hollow-side up, on a serving plate.

2. In an electric mixer fitted with the paddle attachment, beat the mascarpone on medium speed until it is smooth, light, and fluffy, about 2 minutes. Add the confectioners' sugar, vanilla, and a pinch of cinnamon, if using, and beat until fully combined, about 2 minutes.

3. Spoon the mascarpone mixture into a pastry bag fitted with a narrow tip. Alternatively, spoon it into a medium-size plastic bag and snip off a tiny corner to make it function like a pastry bag.

4. Gently squeeze the mascarpone mixture into the hollow center of each strawberry half until it is filled.

make-ahead tips: The sweetened mascarpone filling can be made ahead of time and kept in the refrigerator. Fresh strawberries have a short shelf life so it is best to fill them just before serving.

variation ideas: Drizzle the filled berries with melted dark or white chocolate to make these extra fancy. Or, beat two teaspoons of cocoa powder into the mascarpone to make them chocolate-stuffed strawberries.

savory cheese-pecan biscuits

My friend Nicole and I exchange recipes on a weekly basis. Last year I was searching for a savory biscuit recipe and she suggested these: cheesy biscuits spiced with a generous dose of paprika and a crunchy pecan crust. They are easy to slice and bake right before serving and the dough can be made days in advance. She is a busy mom of two and knows that efficiency is key when it comes to entertaining!

naptime stopwatch

20 minutes prep time
20 minutes bake time

makes approximately
4 dozen biscuits

2 cups all-purpose flour, plus more as needed for dusting

1 teaspoon kosher salt

1 teaspoon paprika

¼ teaspoon crushed red pepper flakes

1 cup (2 sticks) unsalted butter, at room temperature

2 cups (8 ounces) grated sharp Cheddar cheese

1½ cups (6 ounces) pecans, finely chopped

1. In a small bowl, combine the flour, salt, paprika, and red pepper flakes and stir together with a whisk; set aside.

2. In an electric mixer fitted with the paddle attachment, cream the butter and cheese until smooth and creamy, about 3 minutes. With the mixer on low, slowly add in the flour mixture and mix until everything is just combined. The dough will be somewhat dry and crumbly, which is okay.

3. Transfer the dough to a lightly floured surface and form into a log 1½ inches in diameter.

4. Spread the pecans on a rimmed cookie sheet and roll the dough log back and forth over the pecans, pressing them gently into the dough with your fingertips to help them stick. Press all of the pecans into the dough, or as many as possible.

5. Wrap the pecan-encrusted dough in plastic and chill in the refrigerator for at least 2 hours or up to overnight.

6. Preheat the oven to 350°F. Line a baking sheet with parchment paper or a silicone liner.

7. Remove the dough from the refrigerator and cut it into slices ¼-inch thick. Place the slices on the baking sheet 1 inch apart and bake them for 15 to 20 minutes, or until the biscuits have puffed up slightly and are set in the middle. Serve warm or at room temperature.

make-ahead tips: These are the ideal snack to have on hand for last-minute company. Make the dough up to a day ahead of time or freeze it far in advance. To freeze the dough, wrap it in two layers of plastic wrap and an outer layer of aluminum foil. Thaw the dough in the refrigerator for at least 6 hours or up to a day before baking.

serving ideas: Cheesy biscuits are great any time of year. Pile them high on a platter for a buffet or arrange them on a plate with cheese and charcuterie for an easy appetizer.

ricotta crostini with balsamic caramelized onions, honey & sea salt

This is one of my go-to make-ahead appetizers. I cook the onions during naptime and assemble the crostini just before guests arrive. I like to use a light wildflower honey when making these. Its mild, sweet flavor complements the onion and cheese without being overwhelming.

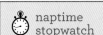 **naptime stopwatch**

10 minutes prep time
20 minutes cook time

makes approximately
25 crostini

1 large baguette

1 teaspoon olive oil

2 large yellow onions, finely chopped

1 pinch kosher salt

4 teaspoons balsamic vinegar

1 ½ cups (12 ounces) fresh ricotta cheese

¼ cup wildflower honey

Sea salt for garnish

1. Preheat the oven to 350°F.

2. Slice the baguette into ½-inch-thick rounds and place them on an ungreased cookie sheet. Toast the rounds in the oven for approximately 8 to 10 minutes, until lightly golden brown, then remove them from the oven and allow them to cool.

3. Set a small skillet over medium-low heat. Add the olive oil, chopped yellow onions, and salt. Cook the onions, stirring continuously, for about 18 to 20 minutes, or until the onions turn a deep brown and are caramelized and crispy around the edges. Stir in the balsamic vinegar and cook for 1 minute more. Remove from the heat and allow the mixture to cool slightly.

4. To assemble, place one heaping teaspoon of ricotta cheese on each round, followed by a teaspoon of the balsamic caramelized onions. Drizzle the top with a small amount of honey and sprinkle lightly with sea salt. Repeat to make the remaining crostini.

make-ahead tips: Caramelize the onions up to a day ahead of time. To reheat them before assembling, warm them in a skillet over medium heat for 2 to 3 minutes, or heat them in the microwave.

summer zucchini bites

I love cooking and baking with fresh zucchini in the summer. I came up with this recipe when I was trying to find ways to use up some leftover grated zucchini from my Chocolate Zucchini Loaf (page 144). Mixing it with a few common pantry staples yielded these light savory bites. They were one of Daphne's first foods, and these days she helps me make them by combining the ingredients with her mini spatula.

naptime stopwatch

15 minutes prep time
18 minutes bake time

makes 24 mini-muffin-sized bites

2 large eggs

2 cups grated zucchini (from 1 medium-to-large zucchini)

½ yellow onion, finely chopped

½ cup (2 ounces) coarsely grated Cheddar cheese

½ cup plain breadcrumbs

¼ cup finely chopped fresh parsley

¼ teaspoon kosher salt

Pinch freshly ground pepper

1. Preheat the oven to 400°F. Butter or spray 1 or 2 mini-muffin tins with nonstick cooking spray and set aside.

2. In a large bowl, lightly beat the eggs with a whisk. Add the zucchini, onion, cheese, breadcrumbs, parsley, salt, and pepper and fold the mixture together using a rubber spatula or wooden spoon. The batter will be sticky and a little loose.

3. Using your hands or a melon baller, fill each muffin cup just to the top, about 1 tablespoon of the mixture.

4. Bake the bites for 15 to 18 minutes, or until the tops are browned and set. The centers of the bites should no longer jiggle when the pan is shaken. Allow the bites to cool in the pan for about 10 minutes, then carefully transfer the bites to a wire rack to cool completely. Repeat for a second batch, if necessary.

make-ahead tips: The zucchini mixture can be made up to 12 hours before it needs to be baked. Once everything is combined, cover the bowl tightly with plastic wrap and place it in the refrigerator. Let the mixture come to room temperature before baking.

variation ideas: To play with the flavor, substitute different hard cheeses for the Cheddar; Gruyère works particularly well. To add more vegetables, reduce the amount of zucchini to 1 cup and add a second cup of chopped vegetables of your choosing. Broccoli, cooked corn, or red bell peppers work nicely.

artichoke-lemon pesto with baked lavash chips

Last summer I treated myself to a teeny jar of lemony artichoke pesto from my local gourmet shop. I could easily have eaten a jar a day, but in the interest of my wallet I decided to try making my own version. Happily, I discovered that making this lush vegetable spread is very simple and takes less than 10 minutes. Now I make it all the time and especially love to eat it with freshly baked lavash chips sprinkled with flakes of fine sea salt. If I can't find lavash—a thin flat bread often used to make sandwich wraps and found in the bread aisle—I use pita bread instead.

naptime stopwatch

10 minutes prep time
8 minutes bake time

makes 2 1/2 to 3 cups

1 (12-ounce) jar artichoke hearts packed in water, drained

1/2 cup (2 ounces) freshly grated Parmesan cheese

1/2 cup (2 ounces) pine nuts, toasted

2 medium garlic cloves, peeled

Zest and juice of 1 1/2 medium lemons

1/2 cup plus 1 teaspoon extra-virgin olive oil, divided

2 sheets lavash

1/2 teaspoon fine sea salt

1. In a food processor fitted with the blade attachment, add the drained artichoke hearts, Parmesan, pine nuts, garlic cloves, lemon zest, and lemon juice. Pulse about 10 to 12 times, until the ingredients come together but are not completely smooth. Scrape down the sides of the food processor.

2. Pour 1/2 cup of olive oil in a steady stream through the feed tube of the processor and process until a chunky pesto forms, about 15 seconds. To make a smoother pesto, process the mixture for a full minute. Pour the pesto into a bowl that can be sealed tightly and store it in the refrigerator until you are ready to eat it.

3. To make the chips, preheat the oven to 350°F. Brush each side of the lavash sheet with the remaining 1 teaspoon of olive oil and sprinkle with sea salt. Bake the lavash on a baking sheet for 6 to 8 minutes, or until it is golden brown and crispy. Allow the sheets to cool until they can be handled comfortably. Then break them into large pieces for dipping.

make-ahead tips: This spread lasts up to week in the refrigerator or several months in the freezer. To freeze, pack and seal spread into a plastic container or freezer bag, leaving about half an inch of headroom to allow for expansion.

variation ideas: Pecorino Romano will lend a saltier bite if used in lieu of Parmesan. To give it a little heat, add a pinch or two of Grains of Paradise or freshly ground black pepper. Grains of Paradise are a spice similar to peppercorns from West Africa; if you can't find them in your gourmet store, try ordering online.

serving ideas: The versatility of this spread is endless. In addition to serving with chips, it is great as a spread for sandwiches, tossed with hot pasta, or used as a vegetable dip.

real tex-mex guacamole

My friend Mimi grew up in Laredo, Texas. She knows her way around Mexican food and swears that her guacamole is the most authentic. It is now Daphne's favorite dip for quesadillas!

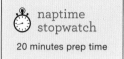
naptime
stopwatch
20 minutes prep time

makes approximately
3 cups

3 medium Haas avocados

Juice of 1 lime

1 medium tomato, seeded
and roughly chopped

½ sweet onion (such as
Vidalia), finely chopped

1 fresh jalapeño, seeded
and finely chopped

2 teaspoons finely chopped
fresh cilantro

1 teaspoon kosher salt

2 tablespoons full-fat sour
cream, stirred well

3 dashes hot sauce, or to taste
(like Tabasco)

1. Halve the avocados, remove the pits, and scoop the flesh into a large mixing bowl. Use the back of a fork to mash the avocado until it is chunky, or to the consistency of your liking. Immediately drizzle the avocado with the lime juice to prevent it from turning brown.

2. Stir the chopped tomato, onion, jalapeño, cilantro, salt, and sour cream into the avocado until they are evenly incorporated. Add the hot sauce and gently stir it into the guacamole. Taste for flavor and add another dash or two of hot sauce if you want it spicier. Serve immediately.

make-ahead tips: To store guacamole, spread plastic wrap over the bowl and press the plastic directly onto the entire surface of the guacamole. This will prevent the top from browning. It will stay fresh in the refrigerator like this for up to 2 days.

serving ideas: This recipe doubles or triples well when serving a crowd. For a true Mexican feel, serve it with fresh tortilla chips and margaritas (page 195).

baked cheese dip

My mom got this simply perfect cheese dip recipe from the chef at The Horned Dorset Inn in Leonardsville, New York, more than twenty years ago. I always adored making it as a special treat when my husband, Duncan, and I were dating. These days I assemble the ingredients during naptime and bake it right before guests arrive.

naptime stopwatch

10 minutes prep time
15 minutes bake time

makes 4 servings

1 large yellow onion, chopped (1 cup)

1 cup good-quality mayonnaise

½ cup (2 ounces) shredded sharp Cheddar cheese

½ cup (2 ounces) shredded Swiss cheese

¼ teaspoon kosher salt

1 pinch freshly cracked black pepper, or to taste

1. Preheat the oven to 350°F.

2. In a large mixing bowl, combine the onion, mayonnaise, both cheeses, salt and pepper and stir with a wooden spoon until everything is combined.

3. Spread the mixture into a small ovenproof dish about 6 inches in diameter or a decorative baking dish of a similar size. Bake the mixture for 10 to 15 minutes, or until the top turns golden brown and the edges are browned and bubbly. Serve immediately.

make-ahead tips: The cheese mixture can be spread in the baking dish and covered tightly with plastic wrap, and stored in the refrigerator for up to 1 day before baking. Bring the cheese mixture to room temperature and remove the plastic wrap before baking.

serving ideas: Assorted crackers, Melba toasts, and baked chips all pair well with this party favorite.

variation ideas: To give this dip some extra heat, add ¼ cup seeded and chopped jalapeños or a pinch of crushed red pepper flakes.

orzo with artichokes, tomato & pine nuts

This is my go-to summer salad and I can guarantee it will become yours, too. It is a snap to pull together and keeps well in the refrigerator. This was one of the first summer recipes I ever posted on my blog and people still leave comments about how much they love it to this day.

naptime
stopwatch

10 minutes prep time
10 minutes cook time

makes 4 servings

1 ½ cups (10 ounces) uncooked orzo

⅓ cup olive oil

¼ cup red wine vinegar

Zest and juice of 1 lemon

1 (9-ounce) bag frozen artichoke hearts, thawed and quartered, or 1 (12-ounce) jar artichoke hearts packed in water, drained and quartered

¼ cup (1 ounce) pine nuts, toasted

1 pint cherry tomatoes, halved

½ teaspoon kosher salt

¼ teaspoon freshly ground black pepper

1. Cook the orzo in a pot of salted boiling water according to package directions. Once the orzo is cooked, drain it and put it in a large bowl.

2. In a small bowl, whisk together the olive oil, vinegar, and lemon zest; set the vinaigrette aside.

3. Add the quartered artichoke hearts and toasted pine nuts to the bowl with the cooked orzo and fold them in until evenly incorporated. Stir the tomatoes into the orzo gently so as not to crush them.

4. Drizzle the vinaigrette evenly over the orzo and toss it lightly to allow it to coat the pasta. Sprinkle the top of the orzo with the fresh lemon juice, season it with salt and pepper, and serve.

serving ideas: Serve up this cold salad alongside fresh Corn on the Cob with Lemon Butter and Salt (page 75) and Spicy Citrus Grilled Shrimp (page 120) for a perfect summer meal.

ruth's curry chicken salad

Ruth was a beloved friend and neighbor, and one heck of a home cook. She used to serve this salad during summer luncheons at her home on Martha's Vineyard. I was enchanted by it at first bite. The flavors are so unique, setting it apart from the ubiquitous deli-style chicken salad. Since Ruth never wrote down a recipe, I asked her to compromise and at least give me the list of ingredients to get me started. She agreed and added a special note at the bottom of her recipe card that always makes me laugh: "The ingredients change a bit depending on the number of martinis I've had when cooking."

 naptime
stopwatch

30 minutes cook time
30 minutes prep time

makes 4 to 6 servings

¼ cup olive oil

1 ½ to 2 pounds skinless boneless chicken breasts, cut into small thin strips

1 large sweet onion (such as Vidalia), finely chopped

4 teaspoons curry powder, divided, plus more to taste

1 ½ cups uncooked basmati rice

2 cups (10 ounces) petite frozen peas, thawed (not cooked)

½ cup golden raisins

⅓ cup roasted unsalted peanuts

⅓ cup sweetened shredded coconut

(continued)

1. In a large sauté pan, warm the olive oil over medium heat and tilt the pan to coat the bottom. Add the chicken strips, onion, and 2 teaspoons of the curry powder. Using a wooden spoon, gently stir the ingredients until the chicken is cooked through and the onion is soft, about 8 to 10 minutes. Using a slotted spoon, remove the chicken and onion from the pan and place them in a large bowl. Allow them to cool to room temperature before assembling the salad.

2. Meanwhile, cook the rice on the stovetop according to package directions. You should have about 4 cups of cooked rice. Allow the rice to cool to room temperature before proceeding.

3. To assemble the salad: Place the basmati rice, chicken, onion, peas, raisins, peanuts, coconut, and scallions in a large bowl. Use a wooden spoon to fold the ingredients together until everything is evenly combined.

4. In a separate bowl, whisk together the mayonnaise, yogurt, cream, salt, and remaining 2 teaspoons of curry powder. If you want the salad to be spicier, add more curry powder pinch by pinch until the mixture suits your taste.

5. Pour the yogurt mixture into the salad and use a wooden spoon or rubber spatula to mix everything together until the yogurt mixture is completely incorporated into the salad and there is none left at the bottom of the bowl. Be sure to mix gently so as not to smash the peas or rice.

make-ahead tips: It is easiest to prepare this salad during naptime, or whenever you have a solid hour of free time. However, you can also break up the recipe by cooking the chicken and rice ahead of time and storing them separately, covered, in the refrigerator. When you are ready to finish the salad proceed with Step 3. The cooked rice and chicken will keep fresh in the refrigerator for up to a day.

serving tips: This is a great recipe for the warmer months when people aren't in the mood for a hot meal. You can easily pack it in take-out boxes for picnics. For summer entertaining, scoop it into a large decorative bowl and serve it with green salad and rolls or mini croissants. If you are serving an especially large group, this recipe doubles well.

variation ideas: The ingredients in this salad are adaptable. If you don't have raisins on hand, chopped apples or sliced grapes can be used instead. Cashews are a tasty substitute for the peanuts.

¼ cup chopped scallions (about 2), white and light green parts only

¼ cup mayonnaise

⅔ cup full-fat Greek yogurt

¼ cup light cream

1 teaspoon kosher salt

couscous salad with
blue cheese & dried cranberries

Couscous is a nice change from cold pasta salad in the summer. The small grains are much less starchy and sticky than noodles when served cold or at room temperature. We often take this sweet, tangy salad with us on boat trip picnics. The variety of contrasting flavors means it is always pairs well with whatever else we have on board. When making use a fruity extra-virgin olive oil; it will transform the dressing.

 naptime
stopwatch

10 minutes cook time
10 minutes prep time

makes 4 servings

1 ½ cups (10 ounces) uncooked plain couscous

⅓ cup extra-virgin olive oil

¼ cup red wine vinegar

Zest and juice of 1 medium lemon

¼ teaspoon kosher salt

1 cup (4 ounces) dried cranberries

1 cup (4 ounces) crumbled blue cheese

½ cup chopped scallions (about 3), white and light green parts only

¾ cup (3 ounces) pecans, coarsely chopped

1. Prepare the couscous according to package directions, making sure to fluff it well with a fork when it's cooked.

2. In a small bowl, whisk together the olive oil, vinegar, lemon zest, lemon juice, and salt. Set aside.

3. Pour the prepared couscous into a large mixing bowl. Add the cranberries, blue cheese, scallions, and pecans and pour the dressing evenly over the top. Mix everything together lightly with a fork so the ingredients are lightly coated with the dressing and the mixture stays fluffy.

4. Taste the salad for seasoning, and add another pinch or two of salt if necessary.

make-ahead tips: This salad tastes better when made ahead; the resting time allows the couscous and cranberries to absorb the flavors of the dressing. I recommend making it at least 2 hours in advance and chilling it, covered, in the refrigerator before serving.

soba noodle salad

This is a terrific cold salad any time of year. I often make a large batch of it during naptime and have some for a late lunch. Then I'll serve the rest of it for dinner topped with Spicy Citrus Grilled Shrimp (page 120) or chicken. I also make this a lot for my friends who are vegan and top it with tofu or steamed bok choy.

 naptime stopwatch

10 minutes cook time
10 minutes prep time

makes 4 servings

8 ounces soba noodles or thin buckwheat noodles

1 tablespoon vegetable oil

1 tablespoon soy sauce

2 teaspoons agave nectar

1 tablespoon rice wine vinegar

¼ cup coarsely chopped scallions (about 2), white and light green parts only

1 tablespoon sesame seeds, lightly toasted

1. Cook the soba noodles according to package directions, then drain and rinse the noodles under cold water to stop the cooking.

2. While the noodles are boiling, whisk together the oil, soy sauce, agave nectar, rice wine vinegar, and scallions in a small bowl.

3. Place the rinsed and drained soba noodles in a large bowl and drizzle the soy sauce mixture over the noodles. Toss the noodles well with tongs or two forks until they are evenly coated with the mixture. Sprinkle the sesame seeds on top as a garnish. Serve in large bowls.

make-ahead tips: This dressing tastes best when mixed about an hour ahead of serving time. The flavors get more complex the longer it sits. Give it a quick whisk before pouring over the noodles.

couscous with tomato & arugula

There are many summer nights when this is our main course. It is so fresh and filling on its own! It is also a great side dish for our favorite grilled foods. It's quick to prepare during naptime, then I dress it with the fresh vinaigrette right before dinner.

**naptime
stopwatch**

10 minutes cook time
10 minutes prep time

makes 4 to 6 servings

1 ½ cups (10 ounces) uncooked plain couscous

½ cup extra-virgin olive oil

Zest and juice of 1 medium lemon

¼ cup red wine vinegar

1 teaspoon kosher salt, divided

1 teaspoon freshly ground black pepper

1 pint grape tomatoes, halved

2 cups (2 ounces) baby arugula, coarsely chopped

1. Prepare the couscous according to package directions, making sure to fluff it well with a fork when it has finished cooking.

2. In a small bowl, whisk together the olive oil, lemon zest, lemon juice, red wine vinegar, salt, and pepper; set the dressing aside.

3. Pour the prepared couscous into a large mixing bowl, add the tomatoes and chopped arugula, and stir well to combine.

4. Drizzle the dressing over the salad and toss it again with a wooden spoon so that the salad is evenly coated.

caprese salad with balsamic syrup

This is a great summer salad that can either be prepared ahead of time or at a moment's notice. I usually make the balsamic syrup in big batches during naptime and use it in pastas and salads all week long. It becomes so concentrated and flavorful when it reduces that there is no need to use pricey balsamic vinegar when making this. I use the basic brand I buy at the grocery store.

naptime stopwatch

15 minutes cook time
10 minutes prep time

makes 4 to 6 servings

1¼ cups balsamic vinegar

2 tablespoons granulated sugar

3 large beefsteak tomatoes, cut into ¼-inch-thick slices

1 pound fresh mozzarella, cut into ¼-inch-thick slices

6 fresh basil leaves, coarsely chopped

½ teaspoon sea salt

1. Bring the balsamic vinegar and sugar to a boil in a small saucepan over medium-high heat. Boil the mixture for about 15 minutes, or until it is reduced to ¼ cup.

2. On a large platter, arrange the tomato and mozzarella slices in an overlapping pattern, alternating a tomato slice with a mozzarella slice.

3. Sprinkle the basil and sea salt over the salad and drizzle the balsamic syrup over the top. Serve immediately.

tri-color salad with parmesan & pine nuts

Green salads are a staple in most homes, including mine. I probably make this salad at least twice a week and we never tire of it. The three types of lettuce give it an unexpected depth of flavor enriched by the mustardy vinaigrette.

naptime stopwatch

15 minutes prep time

makes 6 to 8 servings

1 head endive (about 1½ cups), coarsely chopped

1 head radicchio (about 3 cups), coarsely chopped

7 ounces baby arugula (about 5 cups)

2 tablespoons balsamic vinegar

2 teaspoons Dijon mustard

1 pinch kosher salt

⅓ cup olive oil

⅓ cup (about 1 ounce) coarsely shredded Parmesan cheese

¼ cup (1 ounce) pine nuts, toasted

1. Combine all the lettuces in a large salad bowl and toss them together.

2. In a small bowl, whisk together the balsamic vinegar, mustard, and salt. Pour the olive oil into the bowl in a steady stream, whisking continuously until the mixture is emulsified.

3. Drizzle some of the vinaigrette over the lettuces; add the Parmesan and pine nuts. Toss everything together with large salad tongs. Add more dressing bit by bit if needed.

make-ahead tips: Make large batches of the vinaigrette and store it in the refrigerator. It will last for up to 2 weeks in a sealed container.

variation ideas: To give the salad extra flavor, add some crumbled goat cheese and dried cranberries.

side dishes & vegetables

lazy mom's cheese soufflé

Soufflés are delicious, but they can't usually be prepared ahead of time. When my mother-in-law gave me the recipe for this custardy egg-and-cheese casserole it was the answer to my prayers. It has the creamy texture and airy filling of a soufflé while being nearly as stable as a bread pudding. Plus, it can be assembled far in advance. After it bakes, I take it straight to the table. The puffy top hat of golden cheese always looks so impressive! Be sure to use good quality pre-sliced country bread when making this and pack it in tightly as instructed: it will make all the difference.

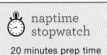

naptime stopwatch

20 minutes prep time
50 minutes bake time

makes 4 to 6 servings

Unsalted butter, as needed

2 tablespoons dried minced onion

1 tablespoon kosher salt

1 teaspoon freshly ground black pepper

6 slices white country bread

1 pound Gruyère cheese, coarsely shredded

4 large eggs

3 cups whole milk

1 teaspoon Worcestershire sauce

1 teaspoon dry mustard powder

1. Butter the bottom and sides of a 2-quart round casserole dish. In a small bowl, stir together the dried onions, salt, and pepper and set aside.

2. Fit 2 slices of the bread into the bottom of the casserole dish. I usually place the bottom edges of the bread together so that the rounded tops of the bread slices fit nicely in the rounded edges of the casserole. It is okay to cut them in order to make them fit, just make sure to pack the bread in tightly and cover the bottom of the dish as much as possible.

3. Sprinkle one-third of the cheese on top of the bread slices. Top this with one-third of dried onion, salt, and pepper mixture. Top with another 2 slices of tightly packed bread and repeat layering until there are 3 layers of bread and three layers of cheese. The third cheese layer should be level with the very top of the dish. Press down firmly on the top of everything to pack it tightly.

3. In a large bowl, whisk together the eggs, milk, Worcestershire, and mustard until blended. Pour this mixture over the casserole slowly, allowing it to soak into the bread and cheese.

4. Cover the dish with plastic wrap and chill in the refrigerator for at least 4 hours or up to 24 hours. Remove it from the refrigerator at least 2 hours before baking (after it has chilled for 4 hours), to allow it to reach room temperature.

5. Preheat the oven to 325°F. Bake the soufflé for 50 minutes, or until the top is puffed up and the cheese is browned. The top will deflate a few minutes after being taken out of the oven, so be prepared to serve it immediately.

make-ahead tips: Ideally, this casserole should be assembled up to a day before it is baked. Assemble it during naptime one day and bake it for the dinner the following night. If you want to bake it the same day, make sure it has chilled for at least 4 hours before being brought to room temperature to bake.

variation ideas: Make this a heartier dish by adding some cooked cubed ham or chopped tomatoes to each layer. This will take it from cheesy side dish to main course!

serving ideas: The most brilliant part about this casserole is the top hat that appears the moment it's taken out of the oven. This moment is fleeting, so take it straight to the table for everyone to admire before it deflates.

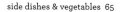

baked sesame tomatoes

This is a fun way to eat summer tomatoes because baking them concentrates their flavor, making them sweeter and chewier. The sesame seeds give them an unexpected crunch and subtle nutty flavor. I often serve them as side dishes in the summer or layered with thinly sliced mozzarella for a light lunch.

 naptime stopwatch

10 minutes prep time
20 minutes bake time

makes 4 servings

4 medium ripe tomatoes

1 teaspoon kosher salt

1 teaspoon garlic powder

¾ cup plain breadcrumbs

2 tablespoons extra-virgin olive oil

1 teaspoon finely chopped fresh oregano

1 teaspoon finely chopped fresh parsley

1 tablespoon sesame seeds

1. Preheat the oven to 400°F.

2. Using a sharp paring knife, cut out the cores of the tomatoes. Slice each tomato in half horizontally and scoop out the seeds. Place the halves cut-side up in a 13 x 9-inch rimmed baking sheet or casserole dish.

3. In a small bowl, mix together the garlic powder and salt and sprinkle the mixture evenly over the tops of the tomatoes.

4. In a separate bowl, mix together the breadcrumbs, olive oil, oregano, parsley, and sesame seeds until crumbs form. Spread this mixture evenly over the tops of the tomatoes.

5. Bake the tomatoes for 20 to 25 minutes, until they are tender enough to be pierced easily with a fork but still hold their shape. Serve hot.

make-ahead tips: These tomatoes can easily be prepared up to a day ahead of time and refrigerated until baking. Bring them to room temperature prior to putting them in the oven.

serving ideas: A platter of these tomatoes is the perfect accompaniment to grilled fish or chicken.

slow-roasted tomatoes

When I bring home way too many tomatoes from the farmer's market the first thing I do is slow-roast a dozen or two. Preparing them barely takes 10 minutes and they don't require any monitoring once they are in the oven. Slow-Roasted Tomatoes can be substituted for the ones in the Homemade Marinara Sauce (page 211) to make a really special sauce, or for the tomatoes in the Caprese Salad with Balsamic Syrup (page 60). We recently discovered they make a great topping for pizza!

naptime stopwatch

10 minutes prep time
3 hours cook time

makes about
4 to 6 servings

1 dozen tomatoes (plum, beefsteak, or heirloom), quartered, stems and cores removed

6 garlic cloves, unpeeled

Olive oil

Kosher salt

1. Preheat the oven to 250°F. Line an 18 x 13-inch jelly roll pan with aluminum foil that extends up and over the edges of the pan.

2. Place the tomatoes cut-side up on the prepared baking pan and scatter the unpeeled garlic cloves around the pan. Drizzle everything with olive oil until all of the tomatoes are lightly coated with a slick of oil. Sprinkle 2 or 3 large pinches of kosher salt over the tomatoes and garlic.

3. Place the pan on the middle rack in the oven and roast the tomatoes for about 3 hours or until tomatoes are shriveled and lightly browned with a little bit of juice and oil gathered in the center.

herbed rice

I discovered this technique of adding dried herbs one night when I couldn't bear the thought of eating plain white rice but had no time to dash to the store. It turns out that adding dried herbs to rice while it cooks is like making your own spice packet. There are infinite flavor possibilities and it is so much tastier than anything store-bought. Now I love to experiment with different herb combinations, always trying new flavors based on what we are having for dinner.

naptime
stopwatch

5 minutes prep time
25 minutes cook time

makes 3 to 4 servings

1 tablespoon unsalted butter

1 cup uncooked jasmine rice

2 ½ cups low-sodium chicken stock

½ teaspoon dried thyme

1 teaspoon dried basil

½ teaspoon dried minced onion

½ teaspoon kosher salt

¼ teaspoon freshly ground black pepper

1. Melt the butter in a medium saucepan over medium heat. Once it has just melted, add the rice and stir it around with a wooden spoon for 1 minute, or until the rice is coated with the butter and lightly toasted.

2. Carefully pour the chicken stock into the pot, then add the thyme, basil, onion, salt, and pepper and stir it briefly so that everything is evenly incorporated and the rice is not sticking to the bottom of the pan.

3. Increase the heat to medium-high to bring the rice to a boil and allow it to boil for 1 minute. Then reduce the heat to low, cover the pot and simmer for about 22 to 25 minutes, or until the rice is tender and the liquid has been absorbed. Fluff the rice with a fork and serve.

make-ahead tips: Mix the dried herbs, salt, and pepper in a ramekin and keep it by the stove. When you begin cooking the rice, it will be ready to use.

serving ideas: Fragrant rice pairs well with all kinds of foods. I often serve it alongside my Roasted Salmon with Herbed Crème Fraîche (page 122) or Perfect Beef Tenderloin (page 135).

asparagus with feta vinaigrette

I am always searching for new ways to prepare fresh asparagus. Once, on a whim, I tossed it with a tangy feta vinaigrette and it was an instant success at the dinner table. Now I make it whenever asparagus is in season, preparing the vinaigrette during naptime and drizzling it over blanched asparagus right before we are ready to dig in. This works best with thick spears of asparagus; they are more flavorful and fun to eat.

 naptime stopwatch

10 minutes cook time
10 minutes prep time

makes 4 servings

1 ¼ teaspoons kosher salt, plus more as needed

2 pounds fresh asparagus

3 tablespoons red wine vinegar

2 tablespoons Dijon mustard

¼ teaspoon freshly cracked pepper

2 tablespoons good-quality olive oil

½ cup (2 ounces) crumbled feta cheese

1. Fill a medium saucepan or deep sauté pan with water halfway up the sides and bring to a boil. Once boiling, add 1 teaspoon of salt to the water.

2. While the water is coming to a boil, prepare an ice bath in a large bowl and set aside.

3. Trim the asparagus by snapping off the tough bottom of each stalk where it naturally breaks when bent. Add the asparagus to the boiling water and cook for 3 to 5 minutes, or until the asparagus is tender enough to be speared through with a fork. Drain the water and plunge the hot asparagus into the ice bath for 30 seconds. Remove the asparagus and drain on a clean kitchen towel.

4. While the asparagus is cooking, whisk together the vinegar and mustard in a small bowl, then add the remaining ¼ teaspoon salt and pepper and allow the salt to dissolve. Pour the olive oil in a thin stream into the mustard mixture, whisking constantly until everything is fully emulsified. Fold the crumbled feta into the dressing with a rubber spatula and set aside. If the dressing separates a little, stir it together again before serving.

5. Place the asparagus in a serving bowl or plate and evenly drizzle with the vinaigrette; toss lightly with a spoon or fork to make sure all of the asparagus is coated. Serve immediately.

make-ahead tips: The asparagus can be blanched a few hours in advance. The feta vinaigrette can also be made up to a day ahead of time. When you are ready to serve the dish, simply bring the asparagus to room temperature and bring everything together as outlined in Step 5.

baked eggplant with goat cheese & tomatoes

My friend Mary gave me the idea for this eggplant preparation while we were standing around the baskets of fresh eggplant at the Cooperstown Farmer's Market. She never prepares it the same way twice, always adding in more vegetables or cheese depending on what is in season. It is such a simple dish that showcases the flavors of fresh summer produce cloaked in a layer of garlic-infused olive oil and is easy to prepare ahead of time!

 naptime
stopwatch

20 minutes prep time
30 minutes cook time

makes 4 to 6 servings

6 garlic cloves, minced

¹/₃ cup coarsely chopped fresh basil

2 teaspoons kosher salt, divided

²/₃ cup olive oil

5 to 6 baby eggplants (about 1 to 1 ¼ pounds), sliced into ¼-inch-thick rounds

1 medium tomato, seeded and cut into ½-inch pieces (about 1 cup)

1 (4-ounce) log herbed goat cheese, crumbled

1. Preheat the oven to 375°F.

2. Add the minced garlic, chopped basil, and 1 teaspoon kosher salt to a large mixing bowl and pour in the olive oil. Stir the mixture briefly so that everything is blended. Add the eggplant slices to the bowl and toss them with the garlic-olive oil mixture, making sure the slices are evenly coated with the garlic and herbs.

3. In a 9 x 9-inch baking dish, layer the coated eggplant slices, letting them overlap a little bit so that they fit snugly in the dish. Drizzle any extra garlic and olive oil from the bowl over the eggplant slices.

4. Scatter the cubed tomatoes on top of the eggplant, followed by the crumbled goat cheese and the remaining teaspoon salt.

5. Bake for 35 to 40 minutes, or until the eggplant is softened and the cheese is slightly melted. Serve hot.

make-ahead tips: This dish can be assembled in its entirety ahead of time and chilled in the refrigerator, covered with plastic, until dinner.

creamy parmesan & chive polenta

Creamy, soft polenta is like nursery food for adults. My favorite way to punch up the flavor of this comforting dish is by adding a generous dose of Parmesan and lots of fresh chives. Since I didn't want to give up polenta after Daphne was born, I learned how to make it ahead and reheat it. It is surprisingly simple to do and is so much easier than stirring a sputtering pot of polenta over a hot stove while trying to entertain a baby.

naptime
stopwatch

25 minutes cook time

makes 4 to 6 servings

4 ½ cups low-sodium chicken stock, divided

1 cup medium-grind polenta or corn grits

2 teaspoons kosher salt

1 teaspoon freshly ground black pepper

¼ cup finely chopped fresh chives

¼ cup whole milk

2 tablespoons unsalted butter

1 cup (4 ounces) freshly grated Parmesan cheese

1. In a large saucepan, bring 4 cups of the chicken stock to a boil over medium-high heat. Reduce the heat to a simmer and add the polenta, stirring as you pour it in to break up any lumps.

2. Adjust the heat so that the polenta remains at a simmer and add the salt, pepper, and chives. Use a long-handled wooden spoon to stir continuously as everything is added, scraping the bottom of the pan from time to time to keep the polenta from sticking to the bottom. Continue to stir until the polenta is thickened, about 15 minutes.

3. Once the polenta is smooth and thickened, turn off the heat and stir in the milk, butter, and Parmesan. Taste for seasonings and add one or two more pinches of salt if needed. If eating right away, pour the hot mixture into a heat-proof bowl and serve hot.

make-ahead tips: Store cooked polenta in the refrigerator—still in its saucepan—covered with plastic wrap. To reheat it, place it back on the stovetop over medium heat and pour in ¼ to ½ cup of additional chicken stock and stir the polenta until it is creamy and heated through.

variation ideas: For some fun variations, try using a nuttier cheese like Gruyère, or spice it up with a few pinches of chili powder to add some heat.

ratatouille

I've always thought that ratatouille is one of the best ways to eat vegetables. I often use this easy technique to make a large batch during naptime when I have loads of fresh vegetables from the farmer's market. I am able to serve it all week in different dishes. Sometimes I stir it into noodles to make a chunky pasta sauce, or use it as a dip or sandwich spread.

naptime stopwatch

20 minutes prep time
1 hour cook time

makes 6 to 8 servings

1 (1 ½-pound) eggplant

3 tablespoons plus 1 teaspoon olive oil, divided

1 medium yellow onion, finely chopped

2 garlic cloves, minced

2 medium red bell peppers, chopped

1 medium zucchini, chopped

1 medium yellow squash, chopped

1 teaspoon coarsely chopped fresh thyme

1 teaspoon coarsely chopped fresh basil

1 teaspoon kosher salt

1 teaspoon freshly ground black pepper

1 small tomato, chopped (about ½ cup), drained of juices

1. Preheat the oven to 400°F. Rub the eggplant lightly with 1 teaspoon of olive oil and prick the skin a few times with the tines of a fork. Place eggplant on a rimmed baking sheet and roast it for 1 hour.

2. Meanwhile, in a large skillet over medium heat, sauté the onion in the remaining 3 tablespoons of olive oil until it is soft and translucent, about 5 minutes. Then add the garlic and cook for 1 minute, stirring with a wooden spoon to make sure it doesn't burn. Reduce the heat to medium-low and add the peppers, zucchini, squash, thyme, basil, salt, and pepper. Cook everything for about 10 minutes, stirring occasionally. Then add the tomato and cook the vegetables for 5 more minutes, or until they are tender and fragrant. Pierce the vegetables with a fork to make sure they are cooked through, transfer the vegetable mixture to a serving bowl and allow it to cool.

3. When the eggplant has finished roasting, it should be collapsed and soft. Remove it from the oven and allow it to cool until it can be handled comfortably. Halve the eggplant and scoop out the flesh with a spoon and place it in a food processor fitted with the blade. Purée the roasted eggplant until it is completely soft, then pour it into the vegetable mixture and stir everything together. Taste for seasonings and add more salt if necessary. Serve immediately or chill, covered, in the refrigerator. Resist the temptation to heavily salt the ratatouille at the outset; the flavors will intensify as it rests in the fridge.

make-ahead tips: This ratatouille lasts for a few days in the refrigerator and is wonderful to have around on days when there isn't much time to cook. With this in the fridge there is always the basis for a good meal ready to go!

serving ideas: Serve this in a big bowl with pita chips for a terrific party dip, on a thick slice of baguette for a light sandwich, or on top of toast with rounds of goat cheese as a tartine. It is also makes an excellent bed for roast chicken or a sauce for pasta.

corn on the cob with lemon butter & salt

There are two ways to cook corn when it's in season and I've given recipes for each method below. When you have the time, light the grill and roast the corn slowly over the open flame. This imparts a sweet, smoky flavor to the kernels, making each bite a succulent treat. Boiling the corn is a faster, more efficient cooking method and is great for hectic nights. Best of all, you can leave the cooked corn in the hot water for up to 30 minutes so people can grab and go as they please.

naptime stopwatch

5 minutes prep time
15 minutes cook time

makes 6 ears

6 tablespoons unsalted butter, at room temperature

Zest and juice of 1 medium lemon

6 fresh ears of corn

1 teaspoon kosher salt

1. *To make the lemon butter:* Use an electric mixer to beat together the butter, lemon juice, and lemon zest in a bowl. Set aside.

2. *To boil the corn:* Shuck the ears of corn and remove all the silk strands. Bring a large pot of salted water to a boil over high heat and add the corn. Boil the corn for 7 minutes, starting to time the cooking after the water has returned to a boil. Remove the corn with tongs and pat dry. Using a knife or spoon, rub some of the lemon butter over the hot kernels, allowing the butter to melt into them and drip onto the plate. Rotate the ear so that all of the kernels are coated. Sprinkle a pinch of salt over the buttered corn and serve immediately.

3. *To grill the corn:* Remove the silk from the tips of the corn ears but keep the rest of the husk intact. Fill a large pot or the kitchen sink with cool water and soak the corn for 20 to 30 minutes. It sometimes helps to place a heavy object over the corn to keep it entirely submerged in the water while it soaks. While the corn is soaking, heat a grill to a medium flame. Remove the corn from the water and shake the excess water off, but don't dry it. Place the wet corn on the hottest part of the grill and cook, turning it occasionally, for 15 minutes. The husks will get brown and have grill marks. To test for doneness, peel back the very top of the husk and press on the kernels. They should be tender to the touch, soft enough that they indent when you press on them. Remove the corn from the grill and let cool for a few minutes until they are comfortable to touch. Peel back the husks entirely and rub the lemon butter across the kernels, allowing the butter to melt into them and drip on the plate. Sprinkle a pinch of salt over the buttered corn and serve immediately.

make-ahead tips: Boiled corn will stay warm in the cooking water for up to 30 minutes. Alternatively, the corn can be boiled at any time of day and cut off the cob to save for a later time. To store cooked corn kernels, allow them to cool to room temperature and keep them in a plastic bag or container in the refrigerator.

variation ideas: To make different flavored butters, add lime zest, orange zest, or a pinch of smoked paprika. Herbed Salt (page 81) would taste great, too.

green beans with toasted almonds, olive oil & sea salt

I developed this particular recipe after eating something similar at a restaurant. The olive oil and sea salt highlight the flavors of the fresh beans, while the lightly toasted almonds give it just the right amount of crunch. I find it easier to make if I cook the beans during naptime then toss them with the oil, salt, and almonds right before dinner. It saves so much time in the evening and still tastes amazing!

naptime stopwatch

2 minutes cook time
10 minutes prep time

makes 4 to 6 servings

Kosher salt for the cooking water

1 pound haricots verts or green beans, trimmed

½ cup (2 ounces) sliced almonds, lightly toasted

½ teaspoon sea salt

3 tablespoons extra-virgin olive oil

1. Fill a large saucepan three-quarters full with water, add a few pinches of kosher salt, and bring it to a boil over medium-high heat. Prepare an ice bath in a large bowl and set aside. Add the trimmed beans to the boiling salted water and make sure that there is enough water to cover the beans. If not, pour in a little more warm water until the beans are covered.

2. Cook the beans in boiling water until they are tender enough to be speared through with a fork but still have a little bit of crunch when you bite into one, about 2 minutes. Then drain the hot water and transfer the beans into the ice bath to shock them. Swish the beans around in the cold water for about 30 seconds then remove them to a clean dish towel to drain; pat dry.

3. Transfer the beans to a large bowl, toss them with the toasted almond slices, sea salt, and olive oil to coat the beans evenly, and serve.

make-ahead tips: Prepare the beans and toast the almonds in advance, but chill the beans and let the cooled almonds sit, covered, at room temperature. At dinnertime, bring the beans to room temperature and toss them with the olive oil, salt, and almonds right before serving.

serving ideas: This recipe doubles or triples well for a crowd and travels well. It is always a great alternative to a green salad and pairs well with Apricot-Mustard Glazed Ham (page 132) or Perfect Beef Tenderloin (page 135).

Opposite page, clockwise from top: Roasted Carrots with Thyme, page 79; Green Beans with Toasted Almonds, Olive Oil & Sea Salt, this page; Sugar Snap Peas with Parmesan and Pine Nuts, page 78

sugar snap peas with parmesan & pine nuts

I make my own Parmesan-pine nut "breadcrumbs" and toss them into dishes when they need a little extra crunch. One day I added them to some freshly sautéed sugar snap peas and they added a welcome salty bite to an everyday side.

naptime stopwatch

5 minutes cook time
10 minutes prep time

makes approximately
4 servings

½ cup (2 ounces) pine nuts, toasted

½ cup (2 ounces) freshly grated Parmesan cheese

1 tablespoon olive oil

1 pound sugar snap peas, washed and patted dry

1 teaspoon freshly ground black pepper

1. Add the pine nuts and Parmesan cheese to a food processor fitted with the blade attachment and pulse until the mixture is finely chopped and resembles coarse breadcrumbs. Set aside.

2. Warm the olive oil in a skillet over medium-high heat. When the olive oil is hot but not smoking, add the peas and toss them in the oil until they are cooked through, but not limp, approximately 5 minutes. This will not take long so keep a constant eye on them.

3. Once the peas are cooked, remove the skillet from the heat and sprinkle in the pine nut mixture and the pepper. Toss everything lightly with a wooden spoon and serve immediately.

make-ahead tips: This recipe doubles or triples well. To make dinner time a snap prepare the Parmesan pine nut mixture ahead of time so it is ready to be tossed in the pan once the peas have been cooked!

roasted carrots with thyme

Roasting carrots with fresh herbs is one of our family favorites and I make them this way a lot. During naptime, I toss the carrots with the seasoning and keep them covered in the fridge until it is time to roast them for dinner.

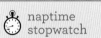

naptime stopwatch

10 minutes prep time
30 minutes cook time

makes 4 servings

2 pounds carrots, peeled and cut into 2-inch pieces

1 tablespoon olive oil

2 teaspoons fresh thyme leaves

2 teaspoons kosher salt

1 teaspoon freshly ground black pepper

1. Preheat the oven to 400°F. Line a large baking sheet with aluminum foil and set aside.

2. In a large mixing bowl, toss together the carrots, olive oil, thyme, salt, and pepper. Spread the carrots evenly on the prepared baking sheet and bake for about 30 to 35 minutes, or until they are softened and lightly brown, stirring with a wooden spoon at 15 minutes to ensure even roasting.

maple-roasted acorn squash
with parmesan-panko topping

Acorn squash is one of our favorite fall vegetables. It's easy to prepare the components ahead of time, then combine them right before dinner. We love this savory, piping hot squash so much that many nights it is our main course with Green Beans with Toasted Almonds (page 76) on the side.

 naptime
stopwatch

20 minutes prep time
1 hour cook time

makes 8 servings

2 tablespoons unsalted butter, melted and divided

1 tablespoon Grade A pure maple syrup

1 large acorn squash

1 teaspoon kosher salt, divided

½ cup (2 ounces) freshly grated Parmesan cheese

½ cup panko breadcrumbs

1. Preheat the oven to 375°F.

2. Melt the butter and allow it to cool slightly. In a small bowl, add 1 tablespoon of the butter to the maple syrup and stir to blend. Set aside.

3. Carefully cut the squash in half lengthwise and remove the seeds and stringy insides. Cut each half into 4 evenly sized wedges and place them skin-side down in a baking dish. Use a basting brush to brush each wedge with the maple syrup butter, so that it is evenly coated. Sprinkle the squash with ½ teaspoon kosher salt.

4. In a small bowl, mix together the Parmesan, panko, the remaining ½ teaspoon kosher salt, and the remaining melted butter.

5. Roast the squash in the baking dish for 30 minutes, then remove the dish from the oven. Place the dish on a stable surface and pack the top of each quarter of squash with the Parmesan-panko mixture. Return the dish to the oven and roast for another 30 minutes, or until it can be pierced easily with a fork. Allow to cool for 5 minutes, and serve warm.

make-ahead tips: The maple syrup butter and Parmesan cheese mixture can both be prepared up to a day ahead of time and stored in the refrigerator until the squash is ready to be basted and cooked.

roasted potatoes
with herbed salt

To give more flavor to our favorite crispy potatoes, I made an herbed salt using dried herbs from my pantry. I like to make the salt in double or triple batches during naptime and then toss some of it with the potatoes right before I roast them. Having the salt ready at dinner is a huge time-saver and is great to use in other dishes, too!

naptime stopwatch

10 minutes prep time
35 minutes bake time

makes 4 to 6 servings

2 teaspoons finely chopped dried rosemary

2 teaspoons finely chopped dried thyme

2 teaspoons finely chopped dried parsley

1 tablespoon kosher salt

1 teaspoon freshly ground black pepper

Zest of 1 medium lemon

3 pounds new potatoes, quartered

3 tablespoons olive oil

1. Preheat the oven to 425°F. Line a rimmed baking sheet with aluminum foil and set aside.

2. Combine all the herbs in a small bowl. Add the salt, pepper, and lemon zest, stirring it all together with a fork until evenly combined.

3. Place the quartered potatoes in a large mixing bowl and drizzle the olive oil over them. Gently toss the potatoes and the oil with your hands or a rubber spatula until the potatoes have a thin, even coating of oil. Sprinkle the herbed salt over the potatoes and toss them again until it evenly coats the potatoes and no salt remains at the bottom of the bowl.

4. Spread the salted potatoes in one even layer on the prepared baking sheet and bake them for 35 to 40 minutes, or until the potatoes are crispy on the outside and soft enough to be speared with a fork.

make-ahead tips: Quarter the potatoes and toss them with the salt ahead of time and refrigerate them, covered with plastic, until you are ready to bake them.

serving ideas: Potatoes often accompany heavier meat dishes like Perfect Beef Tenderloin (page 135) or Apricot-Mustard Glazed Ham (page 132) but can also be enjoyed in the summer alongside a simple dish of Asparagus with Feta Vinaigrette (page 70) for a light lunch.

variation ideas: Nearly any combination of fresh herbs will work with this salt. Use what is available to you and enjoy making up new flavor combinations.

crispy parmesan potato wedges

French fries are always a family favorite but I don't have the time or interest to rig up a deep fryer in the evening, especially when Daphne is bopping in and out of the kitchen. Instead, I make fries at home by tossing them with olive oil and baking them at high heat. Not only does this eliminate the need for hot oil to bubble away on the stovetop, it is also much healthier. We love these, especially served with Uncle Will's Killer Burgers (page 136), or Bistro Steak with Gorgonzola Sauce (page 138). This recipe works really well with sweet potatoes, too.

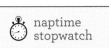

naptime
stopwatch

15 minutes prep time
1 hour cook time

makes approximately
4 to 6 servings

4 russet potatoes, scrubbed
clean

1/3 cup olive oil, divided

2 teaspoons kosher salt
or Herbed Salt (page 81)

2/3 cup (3 ounces) freshly
grated Parmesan cheese

1. Preheat oven to 425°F. Line an 18 x 13-inch jelly roll pan or baking sheet with 1-inch-high sides with aluminum foil and set aside.

2. Cut each potato into 8 wedges and drop them into a 4-quart saucepan. Fill the saucepan three-quarters full with cold water and place on the stove.

3. Bring the water to a boil over medium-high heat and cook the potatoes for about 10 to 12 minutes, or until a fork passes through them but they are still firm, being careful not to overcook. Using a slotted spoon, transfer the potatoes to a colander over the sink to drain, being careful not to break any, and pat them dry with a paper towel.

4. Brush the aluminum foil lined pan with half the olive oil and spread the fries on the foil in one even layer. Brush the tops of the fries with the remaining olive oil and sprinkle them with salt.

5. Bake the fries for 45 minutes, turning every 15 minutes with tongs. While they bake, the edges will start to turn golden brown and the surface will crisp up. At the 45-minute mark, quickly open the oven and sprinkle the Parmesan cheese over the potatoes. Bake for an additional 7 minutes, or until the cheese turns golden brown and melts slightly. Serve hot.

variation ideas: There are almost endless possibilities to flavoring these baked fries. I love to toss them with Herbed Salt (page 81), or add freshly chopped herbs like rosemary, thyme, or basil. Fries are an inherently fun food, so have a great time making up your own flavors!

Opposite page: Uncle Will's Killer Burgers, page 137;
Crispy Parmesan Potato Wedges, this page

steamed artichokes with scallion butter

This was the first way I ever learned to eat artichokes. My mom would serve them with this luxurious dipping sauce and I would happily eat the entire artichoke right down to the heart. These days, I make the sauce ahead of time and cook the artichokes right before dinner.

naptime stopwatch

5 minutes prep time
40 minutes cook time

makes 4 servings

4 large artichokes

1 cup (2 sticks) unsalted butter

½ cup chopped scallions (about 3), white and light green parts only

1 garlic clove, minced

Juice of 1 medium lemon

Pinch kosher salt

Pinch freshly ground black pepper

1. Trim and discard any long stems and cut off the top inch of each artichoke. Use kitchen scissors to cut off any sharp, pointy ends on the leaves. These will not feel good in your mouth!

2. Fill a large pot three-quarters full with water and bring to a boil. Add the artichokes and boil for about 40 minutes, or until the leaves have darkened and are tender enough to be pulled off easily with your fingers. Use tongs to rotate the artichokes in the water every 10 minutes or so to ensure they cook evenly.

3. While the artichokes are cooking, melt the butter in a small saucepan over medium heat. Add the scallions, garlic, lemon juice, salt, and pepper. Stir everything together and keep mixture warm until the artichokes are ready to eat.

4. Serve each artichoke with a dish or ramekin of scallion butter for dipping. Don't forget to carve away the feathery choke from the bottom (or heart) after you've eaten the leaves. The artichoke heart is the best part!

serving ideas: This is a messy dish to eat so only serve it amongst friends. Don't forget to place an extra bowl on the table for the finished leaves and the carved-out choke.

carrot soufflé

My friend Nicole gave me this recipe when we were swapping baby food ideas. But this soft, sweet carrot bake is an adult food that children love, too. It was an instant hit at our dinner table. I don't know who loved it more, my infant or my husband! I still make it all the time. To make it extra fancy for holiday gatherings, I add a sugar-pecan streusel topping.

naptime stopwatch

30 minutes prep time
80 minutes cook time

makes 6 to 8 servings

4 ounces (1 stick) unsalted butter, melted and cooled, plus more for the baking dish

1 pound carrots, peeled and cut into 1-inch pieces

2 cups all-purpose flour

¾ cup granulated sugar

1 teaspoon ground cinnamon

¼ teaspoon freshly grated nutmeg

½ teaspoon kosher salt

2 cups whole milk

1 teaspoon vanilla extract

1. Preheat the oven to 350°F. Butter the bottom and sides of a 13 x 9-inch baking dish and set aside.

2. In a large pot bring 2 quarts of water to a boil over medium-high heat and add the carrots. Cook the carrots until they are tender enough to be easily pierced by a fork, about 10 minutes.

3. While the carrots are cooking, whisk together the flour, sugar, cinnamon, nutmeg, and salt in a large bowl and set aside.

4. When the carrots are cooked, drain them well and add them to a food processor fitted with the blade attachment. Pulse the carrots until they are completely soft and fluffy, almost like mashed potatoes. Add the melted cooled butter and pulse until the mixture is smooth and creamy.

5. Scrape the carrots into the bowl with the dry ingredients and stir until the flour is incorporated into the carrot mixture. Slowly pour in the milk, stirring with a spoon as you do so, and continue stirring until it is completely incorporated.

6. Pour the batter into the prepared pan and bake for 1 hour and 15 minutes, or until the top and edges are golden brown and the soufflé is set in the center. Let cool for 10 minutes before serving.

make-ahead tips: Store the baked soufflé in the refrigerator covered with plastic wrap and reheat it in the oven at 300°F for 15 minutes, or microwave prior to serving.

brussels sprouts with bacon & cranberries

One year, our friends Bernadette and Ray joined us for Thanksgiving on Martha's Vineyard. Bernadette brought a salty-sweet Brussels sprouts dish that we all adored. She had prepared most of it earlier in the day and brought it to the house in a large bowl. Right before dinner she completed the assembly by warming the sprouts in a skillet on the stovetop and adding the cranberries and bacon. I begged her for the recipe and now we make it every Thanksgiving.

naptime stopwatch

20 minutes prep time
20 minutes cook time

makes 6 to 8 servings

6 strips bacon

1 medium yellow onion, finely chopped

2 pounds Brussels sprouts, thinly sliced

1/4 teaspoon kosher salt

Freshly ground black pepper to taste

1/2 cup (2 ounces) dried cranberries

1. Cook the bacon in a large skillet over medium heat until crispy. Using a slotted spoon, transfer the bacon to a plate covered with a paper towel to drain. Once it has cooled enough to touch, crumble it into small pieces and set aside.

2. Drain off all but about 1 tablespoon of the bacon grease. Return the pan to the stove and cook the onion over medium heat until it is soft and translucent, about 6 to 8 minutes. Add the Brussels sprouts and a pinch of salt and pepper to the pan, and cook the sprouts until the edges are crisped and they are cooked through, about 10 to 12 minutes.

3. Scrape the Brussels sprouts into a serving dish and add the crumbled bacon and cranberries. Toss gently and serve.

make-ahead tips: To make this ahead of time, proceed through Step 2 and cook the sprouts for about 8 minutes, then remove the sprouts from the heat. They can later be reheated in a skillet on the stovetop over medium heat for about 2 minutes. Once warmed, toss in the bacon and cranberries and serve hot!

soups & stews

summer gazpacho

This is my favorite recipe for this classic cold soup. It is chock-full of vegetables with just the right amount of heat from a dash of hot pepper sauce. My mother always made it for us growing up, and now I make it nearly every week all summer long. The preparation is very simple. Since it doesn't need to be heated we often take it with us on evening boat picnics. Its cool, refreshing flavor is perfect on hot summer days.

naptime stopwatch

15 minutes

makes 4 to 6 servings

20 ounces (2 ½ cups) regular tomato juice, divided

1 red bell pepper, seeded and quartered

2 scallions, trimmed and washed

2 garlic cloves

1 large cucumber, peeled and cut into 4 evenly sized pieces

3 medium plum tomatoes, seeded and quartered

⅓ cup red wine vinegar

1 teaspoon kosher salt

1 teaspoon freshly ground black pepper

1 tablespoon hot pepper sauce

2 tablespoons olive oil

3 limes, cut in half

1. Add ¾ cup of the tomato juice, the red bell pepper, scallions and garlic to a large food processor fitted with a blade and pulse 3 to 4 times. Add the cucumber and tomatoes and pulse 3 to 4 more times until all of the ingredients are coarsely chopped. Add the red wine vinegar, salt, and pepper and pulse twice. Finally, pour in the remaining tomato juice, hot pepper sauce, and olive oil. Pulse the food processor twice more. The vegetables should be finely chopped, but not liquefied.

2. Chill the gazpacho in a covered container in the refrigerator for at least two hours prior to serving. To serve, divide the gazpacho among 4 to 6 bowls. Squeeze the juice of half a lime over each bowl and stir it into each portion.

variation ideas: If this soup is too spicy for your taste, reduce the amount of hot pepper sauce you use.

chicken sausage & tortellini soup

This is a great sick day soup. At the first sign of the sniffles I whip up a big batch during naptime. One bowlful is guaranteed to alleviate all my aches and pains or at least improve my state of mind. I often make a double batch and freeze half so there is always some around on nights I don't have time to cook!

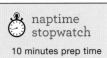

naptime stopwatch

10 minutes prep time
25 minutes cook time

makes 6 to 8 servings

2 tablespoons olive oil

12 ounces organic chicken sausage, casings removed

1 medium yellow onion, finely chopped

3 garlic cloves, minced

1 teaspoon kosher salt

½ teaspoon freshly ground pepper

¼ cup dry white wine

32 ounces (4 cups) low-sodium chicken or vegetable stock

1 (28-ounce) can crushed tomatoes with juices

3 fresh basil leaves, torn

1 (10-ounce) bag cheese tortellini

6 cups (8 ounces) fresh spinach, coarsely chopped

½ cup freshly grated Parmesan cheese, for serving (optional)

1. Warm the olive oil in a heavy stockpot over medium heat. Chop the chicken sausage into bite-sized pieces and add them to the pot. Add the onion, garlic, salt, and pepper and cook until the meat is no longer pink and the onion is translucent, about 5 minutes.

2. While stirring, add the white wine and scrape up any brown bits from the bottom of the pan. Simmer everything over medium heat until the wine has reduced by half, about 2 minutes.

3. Carefully pour in the stock and crushed tomatoes with juices, and add the basil. Bring the soup to a simmer, add the tortellini and simmer for about 10 minutes, or until the tortellini is cooked and floats at the top of the soup. Reduce the heat to medium-low and simmer the soup for an additional 5 minutes, or until it is slightly thickened. Drop in the spinach and cook until the leaves are just wilted, about 2 minutes.

4. Ladle the hot soup into big bowls and top with grated Parmesan cheese if desired.

make-ahead tips: Like most soups, the flavor of this one intensifies and improves with time. This soup also freezes beautifully and transports well. To freeze, pour the completely cooled soup into a sealable plastic container, leaving 1 inch of headspace to allow for expansion. (Mark the container clearly since it can be hard to identify when frozen.) To reheat, bring the sauce to a simmer over medium heat in a saucepan. If it has thickened a lot, add ½ cup of chicken stock to thin it out. Add the Parmesan at the table.

variation ideas: Diced ham, shredded cooked chicken, or ground beef all are excellent substitutions for the chicken sausage. You can also add more veggies, including finely chopped carrots, celery, or fennel.

ham & corn chowder

This hot, creamy soup is the perfect foil for chilly weather. I love to make it during naptime so that it is ready to be reheated and served in the evening. By the time Daphne is out of her snowsuit for the day and the fire is lit, the soup is heated through and ready to eat.

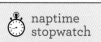

naptime stopwatch

10 minutes prep time
20 minutes cook time

makes 4 to 6 servings

3 medium yukon gold potatoes, peeled and cut into ½-inch cubes

2 carrots, shredded

½ medium yellow onion, chopped

1 teaspoon kosher salt

2 tablespoons unsalted butter

1 (14-ounce) can creamed corn, with liquid

6 ounces cooked ham, cut into ½-inch cubes (1 cup)

1 cup light cream

1 cup whole milk

Pinch freshly ground black pepper

1. In a large heavy saucepan, combine the potatoes, carrots, onion, and salt. Pour in enough water to cover the vegetables and bring to a boil over medium-high heat. Continue boiling until the potatoes are soft enough to be speared with a fork, about 4 to 5 minutes. Remove from the heat and strain the vegetables through a fine mesh sieve. Reserve the liquid as vegetable stock for another use, or discard.

2. Pour the vegetables back into the same pan and add the butter, creamed corn, chopped ham, light cream, milk, and pepper. Warm the soup over medium-low until it is heated through and serve.

make-ahead tips: This soup will keep refrigerated for up to 3 days. After that the vegetables get a little mushy.

serving ideas: We often debate whether to serve this chowder in bowls or mugs. When eating this outside on a brisk fall evening we prefer mugs for ease of carrying them around with us. When casually entertaining, I like to leave it on the stovetop and let people serve themselves right out of the pot.

variation ideas: Cooked ham gives this chowder a salty bite. If you don't have any on hand, use a few freshly cooked strips of bacon or pancetta instead.

four-bean chili mole

My friend Bobby runs the awesome web site Curious Soups and his soup recipes are some of the best around. This is his chili recipe, which was inspired by his favorite Mexican mole sauce. It has a great balance of sweetness and heat from the variety of peppers and the unexpected addition of cocoa powder, a typical flavor in mole.

naptime stopwatch

20 minutes prep time
40 minutes cook time

makes approximately
8 to 10 servings

1 tablespoon canola oil

4 carrots, peeled and sliced into ½-inch pieces

2 medium yellow onions, finely chopped

6 garlic cloves, minced

1 (15-ounce) can kidney beans

1 (15-ounce) can black beans

1 (15-ounce) can pinto beans

1 (15-ounce) can chick peas

1 (28-ounce) can diced tomatoes

1 red bell pepper, coarsely chopped

2 poblano peppers, coarsely chopped

2 serrano peppers, coarsely chopped

(continued)

1. In a heavy large stock pot or Dutch oven, warm the oil over medium heat. When the oil is hot but not smoking, add the chopped carrots and onions and cook for about 5 minutes, until the onions begin to sweat and turn translucent. Add the garlic and stir for another minute, or until the garlic is fragrant.

2. Pour in 6 cups of water and increase the heat to medium-high to bring the water to a boil. While the water is heating up, drain and rinse the kidney beans, black beans, pinto beans, and chick peas and place them in a large mixing bowl. Set aside.

3. Once the water is boiling, add the drained beans, tomatoes and all peppers and bring the chili back to a boil for 1 minute. Then, reduce the heat to medium-low so that the mixture is at a low simmer.

4. Stir in the oregano, chili powder, cocoa powder, cumin, salt, pepper, cilantro, and corn and allow the mixture to simmer for 30 minutes un covered, stirring occasionally.

5. Remove the chili from the heat and ladle it into individual bowls. Dollop each bowl with a heaping teaspoon of sour cream, a garnish of shredded Cheddar cheese, and a sprinkle of fresh cilantro.

1 habañero pepper, coarsely chopped

1 teaspoon dried oregano

2 teaspoons chili powder

4 teaspoons unsweetened cocoa powder

½ teaspoon ground cumin

2 teaspoons kosher salt

2 teaspoons freshly ground black pepper

2 tablespoons fresh cilantro, coarsely chopped, plus more for serving

1 ¾ cups (10-ounce bag) frozen corn kernels, thawed

Sour cream, for serving

Shredded Cheddar cheese, for serving

creamy butternut squash & ginger soup with apple cider

I look forward to making this soup every fall. It's the perfect cold weather meal and the whole house smells amazing after I've spent the afternoon cooking with squash and ginger. For extra flavor, I like to add a touch of apple cider. The natural sweetness mellows the spicy ginger.

 naptime stopwatch

15 minutes prep time
1 hour 20 minutes cook time

makes 8 servings

3 medium butternut squashes
(about 9 pounds total)

½ cup olive oil, divided

½ teaspoon kosher salt,
plus more as needed

¼ teaspoon freshly ground black
pepper, plus more as needed

½ medium yellow onion,
finely chopped

2 garlic cloves, minced

2 tablespoons minced fresh
ginger

1 teaspoon ground cinnamon

5 cups chicken or vegetable
stock

¼ cup heavy cream

1 cup apple cider

1. Preheat the oven to 425°F. Line one or two rimmed baking sheets with aluminum foil.

2. Cut each squash in half lengthwise and scoop out the seeds and stringy flesh. Place the squash halves skin side down on the prepared baking sheets, and generously drizzle 1 tablespoon of olive oil over each half followed by the salt and pepper. Bake for 50 to 60 minutes or until the flesh is tender enough to be pierced with a fork. Allow the squash to cool until it is comfortable enough to handle.

3. Meanwhile, in a heavy large stockpot over medium heat, heat the remaining 2 tablespoons of olive oil. Add the onion, garlic, ginger, and cinnamon and sauté until onion is translucent, about 5 minutes. Slowly pour in the stock, stirring the vegetables as you do so, and bring it to a simmer.

4. Use a large spoon to scoop the soft squash into the soup and use an immersion blender to purée the soup until completely smooth. Alternatively, carefully transfer the soup in batches to a blender and process until smooth. Pour the smooth soup back into the stockpot and proceed.

5. With the heat on low, stir in the cream followed by the apple cider, ½ teaspoon salt, and ¼ teaspoon pepper. Increase the heat and bring the soup briefly to a boil, then reduce the heat and simmer for about 2 minutes, stirring occasionally. Taste for seasonings and add more salt or pepper if needed. Serve hot.

make-ahead tips: Roasting the butternut squash can be done up to a day ahead. Scoop the squash out of the skins and store it in a sealed container in the refrigerator until ready to use. This soup tastes better after it has rested. Try to make it at least 2 or 3 hours before serving it.

serving ideas: For a fun nibble on the side, serve with slices of baguette that have been topped with Gruyère cheese and broiled for a minute or two.

sweet potato & lentil stew

My friend Kristina made this for me during a visit to my apartment in New York City. She'd offered to take care of dinner plans while I was at work. Neither one of us had children at the time, but she still made it during the day while I was gone and reheated it for dinner!

naptime stopwatch

15 minutes prep time
50 minutes cook time

makes 4 to 6 servings

2 tablespoons olive oil

1 medium yellow onion, finely chopped

2 tablespoons fresh ginger, finely chopped

1 garlic clove, minced

2 teaspoons curry powder

1 teaspoon kosher salt

32 ounces (4 cups) low-sodium chicken stock

2 large sweet potatoes, peeled and chopped into 1-inch cubes

1 (14-ounce) can chopped tomatoes with juices

1 cup brown lentils

Freshly ground black pepper (optional)

1. In a heavy stockpot or Dutch oven, heat the olive oil over medium heat. Add the chopped onion and gently sauté until tender, about 5 minutes.

2. Add the ginger, garlic, curry powder, and salt to the pan and stir until the mixture is fragrant, about 2 minutes.

3. Carefully pour in the chicken stock and add the potatoes, tomatoes, and lentils. Increase the heat to medium-high and bring the stew to a boil. Allow it to boil for 1 minute, then reduce the heat to medium-low and simmer everything, stirring occasionally, for about 40 minutes, or until the sweet potatoes are tender enough to pierce easily with a fork. Before serving, taste the soup and add an extra pinch of salt and pepper if necessary. Serve hot!

make-ahead tips: Place the cooled soup in a plastic container and tightly seal. It will keep well in the freezer for up to 2 months. Be sure to clearly mark the container before freezing!

serving tips: Whole wheat pitas cut into wedges are great for enjoying with this stew. I like to toast them until they are almost crispy, then use them to scoop up the stew from the bowl.

paprika pork stew with sour cream

This recipe is one of our favorites from my mom's friend Maryann. My mom made it a lot when we were young and now I make it for my family. It is the perfect cozy stew for cold winter days.

naptime stopwatch

15 minutes prep time
1 hour 45 minutes cook time

makes 4 to 6 servings

2 tablespoons olive oil

1 yellow onion, finely chopped

1 (1 ½- to 2-pound) pork tenderloin, cut into 1-inch pieces

2 tablespoons paprika

1 ½ teaspoons chili powder

2 medium garlic cloves, minced

1 tablespoon all-purpose flour

1 cup low-sodium chicken stock

1 red bell pepper, finely chopped

1 (14-ounce) can crushed tomatoes with juices

1 tablespoon tomato paste

½ teaspoon salt

1 pinch freshly ground black pepper

¼ cup full-fat sour cream

1. In a heavy large pot or Dutch oven, heat the olive oil over medium heat until hot but not smoking. Add the onion and sauté, stirring occasionally, until it is soft and translucent, about 3 minutes.

2. While the onion is cooking, place the pork in a mixing bowl and toss it with the paprika until the meat is evenly coated.

3. Carefully add the pork to the cooked onions and continue cooking until the pork is evenly browned and cooked through, about 8 to 10 minutes. Add the chili powder and the garlic to the pan and sauté for 1 to 2 minutes, or until the garlic is fragrant.

4. Sprinkle the flour over the meat and give it a quick stir to incorporate. Carefully add in the chicken stock, red pepper, crushed tomatoes, tomato paste, salt, and pepper and reduce the heat to medium-low.

5. Cover the stew and simmer stirring occasionally, for about 1 hour and 30 minutes. As it simmers, it will thicken up slightly. Once it has finished cooking, taste it for seasoning and add another pinch or two of salt if needed. Ladle the hot stew into bowls and stir 1 tablespoon of sour cream per bowl to serve.

make-ahead tips: To store the stew, let it cool to room temperature and pour it into an airtight container. It can be store in the refrigerator for up to three days. To reheat the stew, bring it to a simmer over medium-low and cook until heated through. Always wait to stir in the sour cream until just before serving.

main dishes

baked gnocchi with
roasted eggplant & mozzarella

When Duncan and I were dating we always ordered a similar dish at our favorite neighborhood restaurant. When Daphne was born we couldn't frequent this spot nearly as often as we wanted, so I recreated the dish at home. We have since moved out of that neighborhood, but every time we eat this it brings back wonderful memories.

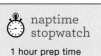 naptime
stopwatch

1 hour prep time
30 minutes cook time

makes 4 to 6 servings

1/3 cup olive oil

1 garlic clove, minced

2 teaspoons kosher salt

1 large eggplant (about
1 pound), chopped into
3/4-inch cubes

1 pound potato gnocchi,
fresh or frozen, thawed
if frozen

8 ounces fresh mozzarella,
cut into 1/2-inch cubes

3 tablespoons coarsely
chopped fresh basil

24 ounces marinara sauce,
store-bought or homemade
(page 211)

1/2 cup (2 ounces) freshly
grated Parmesan cheese

1. Preheat the oven to 400°F. Line a rimmed baking sheet with aluminum foil and set aside.

2. In a large bowl, combine the olive oil, minced garlic, and salt and stir to combine.

3. Add the eggplant cubes to the large bowl with the garlic-olive oil mixture and toss until they are completely coated with the oil and no oil is left pooling at the bottom of the bowl. Spread the eggplant cubes in one even layer on the lined baking sheet and drizzle any remaining olive oil from the bowl over them. Roast the eggplant for about 35 minutes, turning once midway through, until the eggplant is soft and cooked through. Remove it from the oven and allow the cubes to cool until they are comfortable enough to touch. Reduce the oven temperature to 350°F.

4. Meanwhile, pour the gnocchi into a 2-quart baking dish. Add the cubed mozzarella, roasted eggplant, and basil and toss everything gently with a wooden spoon so that it is evenly distributed.

5. Pour the marinara sauce over the gnocchi mixture and spread it with a spoon so that it evenly covers the gnocchi. Sprinkle the top with the Parmesan cheese and bake the gnocchi for 30 to 35 minutes, or until the mixture is hot and bubbly and the gnocchi is cooked through.

make-ahead tips: The eggplant can be roasted in advance if you don't have time to do it right before dinner. The entire casserole can also be assembled in its entirety during naptime and refrigerated until you are ready to bake it that evening.

spinach & ricotta ravioli
with balsamic browned butter

Using wonton skins, ravioli are easy and fun to make during naptime. Once I assemble them I let them dry on the countertop for the afternoon until it is time to cook them for dinner.

naptime stopwatch

25 minutes prep time
10 minutes cook time

makes 4 servings

1 (10-ounce) bag frozen chopped spinach, thawed and drained

1 cup (8 ounces) ricotta cheese

¼ cup (1 ounce) freshly grated Parmesan cheese

1 tablespoon finely chopped fresh parsley

½ teaspoon kosher salt

½ teaspoon freshly ground black pepper

40 wonton skins, thawed if frozen

4 tablespoons (½ stick) unsalted butter

1 teaspoon balsamic vinegar

1. In a medium bowl, mix together the spinach, ricotta, Parmesan, parsley, salt, and pepper.

2. Arrange 20 of the wonton skins in rows on ungreased baking sheets. Spoon 1 heaping tablespoon of the ricotta mixture into the center of each wonton. Fill a small bowl with water and use a small brush or your fingertip to brush the water around all four edges of each wonton skin. Top each wonton with a second wonton skin and press down firmly with your fingertips, then crimp the edges with a rolling crimper or the tines of a fork to seal in the ricotta mixture. Use your fingers to ensure that each one is tightly sealed. Let the ravioli stand at room temperature for at least 30 minutes to dry.

3. Bring a large pot of salted water to a boil and cook the ravioli in two batches, making sure they don't stick together in the water. Boil each batch for about 5 minutes or until the raviolis are translucent and float to the surface, then transfer them to a serving dish.

4. While the last batch is cooking, melt the butter in a small skillet over medium heat. Allow the butter to warm until it is bubbly and turns a golden brown with a nutty fragrance, about 2 to 3 minutes. Keep swirling the pan so that the milk solids don't burn. Remove the browned butter from the heat and whisk in the balsamic vinegar. Drizzle over the ravioli, toss gently to coat, and serve.

make-ahead tips: After the ravioli have dried on the counter for about 5 minutes, they can be stored in the refrigerator on a baking sheet covered with plastic wrap until you are ready to cook them. They can be stored like this for up to 1 day.

pizza with artichokes, caramelized shallots & ricotta

We love making pizza at home. To change up our usual cheese pizza recipe I sometimes make this white pizza topped with our favorite vegetables and cheeses. I caramelize the shallots during naptime and have Daphne help me roll out the dough to put it in the pan right before dinner.

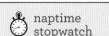
naptime stopwatch

15 minutes prep time
35 minutes cook time

makes 3 to 4 servings

Cornmeal as needed,
for the pan

3 tablespoons good-quality
olive oil, plus more for
brushing the pan

3 tablespoons unsalted butter

1 pound shallots, coarsely
chopped

1 teaspoon kosher salt

All-purpose flour for dusting

8 ounces store-bought pizza
dough

1 ½ cups (6 ounces) freshly
grated fontina cheese

1 (9-ounce) bag frozen
artichoke hearts, thawed
and chopped into bite-sized
pieces

¾ cup (6 ounces) fresh ricotta
cheese

1. Preheat the oven to 425°F. Scatter a light dusting of cornmeal evenly on a pizza stone, or rub a 13 x 9-inch jelly roll pan generously with olive oil and sprinkle cornmeal evenly over the surface of the pan.

2. Melt the butter in a medium skillet over medium heat and add the shallots. Sauté the shallots for about 13 to 15 minutes, stirring often, until they take on a darker brown color, reduce in volume slightly, and become caramelized. Remove from the heat and set aside.

3. Lightly flour a clean work surface and roll out the pizza dough until it is ⅛-inch thick and it fits the shape of the pizza stone or jelly roll pan. Place the pizza on the stone or pan and drizzle the 3 tablespoons olive oil over the dough. Use the back of a spoon to spread it evenly over the surface of the dough. Bake it for about 8 to 10 minutes, or until bubbles start to form on the surface of the dough.

4. Remove the pizza crust from the oven (maintain oven temperature). Scatter the fontina on top of the hot crust. Then layer on the caramelized shallots and chopped artichoke hearts, and dollop the ricotta randomly over the pizza by the tablespoonful.

5. Return the pizza to the oven and bake it for 13 to 15 minutes, or until the cheese is melted, the crust is golden around the edges, and the pizza is piping hot. Cut the pizza into pieces and serve.

variation ideas: Homemade pizza can be tweaked in many different ways. For a simple cheese pizza, add pizza sauce and mozzarella after the dough has baked. Other fun toppings are roasted eggplant, grilled sausage, or asparagus.

pastitsio

My friend Ariana inherited this recipe from her Greek grandmother. I first tasted this creamy baked pasta when she made it for the moms at our kids' playgroup. Poor Ariana: once we all realized how she could cook, she became the most popular playgroup hostess in town!

naptime stopwatch

15 minutes prep time
1 hour 15 minutes cook time

makes 8 servings

pasta and meat sauce

Unsalted butter, as needed

⅓ cup plus 1 teaspoon olive oil, divided

3 small yellow onions, finely chopped

1½ pounds ground beef (85% lean)

⅓ cup dry red wine

1 (14-ounce) can chopped tomatoes with juices

2 cups (8 ounces) coarsely grated Kefalotiri cheese (Parmesan or Romano cheese can be substituted)

1 pound perciatelli pasta (also called bucatini; any long pasta can be substituted)

1. Preheat the oven to 400°F. Butter the bottom and sides of a deep 13 x 9-inch baking dish and set aside.

2. *To make the pasta and meat sauce:* Heat ⅓ cup olive oil in a large pot over medium heat. Add the onions and cook until they are completely translucent, about 3 to 5 minutes. Increase the heat to medium-high, add the ground beef, and cook until it is no longer pink, breaking it apart with a wooden spoon as it cooks.

3. Carefully add the red wine to the beef in the pot and scrape up any browned bits from the bottom of the pan with a wooden spoon. Simmer the mixture until it has reduced by half. Reduce the heat to low, add the tomatoes, and let the mixture simmer on low for about 30 minutes. If it begins to seem too dry, add a small amount of water to loosen it up.

4. Meanwhile, bring a large pot of salted water to a boil and cook the pasta to al dente according to package directions. Drain and set aside to cool slightly. Once the pasta is cool, toss it with the remaining 1 teaspoon olive oil to coat and divide in half.

5. *While the beef is simmering, make the béchamel sauce:* In a large saucepan, melt the butter over low heat then, working quickly, add the flour and whisk it with the butter until it is completely smooth. Keep whisking for 1 minute to cook the flour slightly; the color should still be pale. Increase the heat to medium-high and gradually pour in the milk, stirring constantly so that the mixture stays smooth and everything is fully combined. Keep whisking the sauce until it starts to thicken, but do not let it come to a boil. Once the béchamel coats the back of a spoon, remove it from the heat.

6. Crack the eggs into a small bowl and whisk them together. Add a small amount of the hot milk sauce to the eggs and whisk quickly to combine. This will temper the eggs so that they don't cook when added into the hot béchamel. Pour the egg mixture into the sauce, whisk to

combine it, then add ¾ cup of the grated cheese and stir until it is melted and fully incorporated into the sauce. Stir in the nutmeg, salt and pepper and set aside.

7. Spread half of the cooked pasta on the bottom of the prepared baking dish. Cover it with 1¼ cups of the grated cheese and all of the meat mixture. Top the meat mixture with the remaining half of pasta.

8. Carefully pour the béchamel over the top of the pasta and sprinkle remaining ¼ cup of grated cheese over the top. Place the dish on a baking sheet and bake it for 30 to 35 minutes, or until the top is brown and the cheese is fully melted.

make-ahead tips: This dish reheats well and can easily be made ahead of time. To freeze it, remove the casserole from the dish to a sheet of plastic wrap. Wrap it in a double layer of plastic wrap and an outer layer of aluminum foil. It can be frozen like this for up to 3 months.

béchamel sauce

¼ cup (½ stick) unsalted butter

½ cup all-purpose flour

3 cups whole milk, at room temperature

3 large eggs

1 cup (4 ounces) coarsely grated Kefalotiri cheese (Parmesan or Romano can be substituted), divided

1 pinch freshly grated nutmeg

½ teaspoon kosher salt

½ teaspoon freshly ground black pepper

crunchy mac & cheese with bacon

When I first read Amanda Hesser's recipe for Crunchy Mac & Cheese on food52.com, I couldn't wait to make it. I loved the idea of a mac-and-cheese that is predominantly crunchy with a thin creamy underbelly. To give the recipe some more heft I added panko breadcrumbs for crunch and salty bacon for flavor. The result is this decadent dinner that our whole family loves.

naptime
stopwatch
20 minutes prep time
15 minutes cook time

makes 8 servings

3 tablespoons unsalted butter, divided

1 pound rotini or fusilli pasta

3 cups (12 ounces) extra-sharp Cheddar cheese, coarsely grated

3 cups (12 ounces) sharp Cheddar cheese, coarsely grated

¼ teaspoon dry mustard powder

1 pinch kosher salt

8 strips good-quality bacon, cooked and coarsely chopped

1 cup panko breadcrumbs, divided

⅔ cup whole milk

1. Preheat the oven to 475°F.

2. Use 1 tablespoon of the butter to thickly grease a 17 x 11-inch jelly roll pan. Make sure every inch is covered.

3. Bring a large pot of salted water to a boil, add the pasta, and cook it for 6 minutes; the pasta will still be slightly underdone. Drain and set aside.

4. While the pasta is cooking, combine the grated cheeses in a large heatproof bowl and scoop out 2 cups to reserve for the topping.

5. Working quickly, pour the drained pasta into the heatproof bowl with the cheese, then add the mustard, a pinch of salt, the bacon pieces, and ½ cup of panko. Toss the mixture until the pasta is evenly coated with the bacon pieces and the cheeses.

6. Spread the pasta mixture in one even layer onto the buttered pan and pour the milk evenly over the surface of the pasta. Then top the pasta with the reserved 2 cups of cheese and ½ cup of panko and dot the top with the remaining 2 tablespoons butter. Bake the pasta for 15 minutes, or until the crust of the cheese is golden and crisp. Serve it hot or reheat it in the oven for 5 minutes at 350°F before serving.

make-ahead tips: To speed up assembly in the evening, shred the cheeses during the day.

variation ideas: For a plain mac-and-cheese, omit the bacon. Plain breadcrumbs may be used if panko is unavailable.

artichoke lasagna

This recipe was inspired by my friend Barbara. She had adapted the Marcella Hazan recipe of the same name to be much simpler for home cooks. After I tasted Barbara's version I fell in love and started making it regularly, especially in the colder months when we're in the mood for rich, creamy meals. I can assemble the entire lasagna during naptime and refrigerate it until I am ready to bake it for dinner.

naptime stopwatch

15 minutes prep time
1 hour cook time

makes 8 to 10 servings

4 ½ ounces (9 tablespoons) unsalted butter, divided, plus more for the baking dish

3 garlic cloves, minced

½ teaspoon crushed red pepper flakes

3 (9-ounce) bags frozen artichoke hearts, thawed and quartered

½ cup dry white wine

Juice of 1 lemon

6 tablespoons all-purpose flour

2 ½ cups whole milk

½ cup low-sodium chicken stock

1 teaspoon kosher salt

1 teaspoon freshly ground black pepper

1 ½ cups (6 ounces) freshly grated Parmesan cheese

1 (12-ounce) box no-boil lasagna noodles

1. Preheat the oven to 350°F. Lightly butter the bottom and sides of a deep 13 x 9-inch baking dish and set aside.

2. In a large sauté pan over medium heat, melt 3 tablespoons of butter and add the garlic, red pepper flakes, and artichoke hearts. Sauté everything for about 4 minutes, or until the artichokes are tender and the butter is completely absorbed. Then pour in the white wine and lemon juice and allow it to simmer until the liquid is reduced by half. Remove the pan from the heat and set aside.

3. In a deep saucepan, melt the remaining 6 tablespoons of butter over medium-low heat. Once the butter is melted, add the flour and whisk the mixture constantly for about 2 minutes to make sure the roux doesn't burn. Slowly pour the milk into the pan, stirring continuously to break up any lumps of flour. Carefully add the chicken stock and stir the mixture over medium heat for about 8 to 10 minutes, or until the sauce thickens enough to coat the back of a spoon. Add the salt and freshly ground pepper and taste for seasonings; add a pinch or two more of salt if needed.

4. Pour a small amount of sauce into the baking dish to cover the entire bottom and arrange 3 noodles on top of it. On top of the noodles pour half of the sautéed artichokes, followed by one-third of the sauce and one-third of the Parmesan cheese. Repeat these steps to form a second layer. Place the third layer of noodles on top of the lasagna and pour the remaining third of the sauce evenly over them, topped with the remaining Parmesan.

5. Bake the lasagna for 45 to 50 minutes, or until the top is browned and the sauce is bubbly. Allow the lasagna to rest for about 10 minutes on the counter to firm up. Slice and serve.

make-ahead tips: Assemble the lasagna during the day and refrigerate, covered, until you are ready to bake it. Bring it to room temperature before baking. Leftovers can easily be reheated and enjoyed for a few days after you make it.

brown butter asparagus risotto

We love risotto but it can take some time to pull together for dinner. After Daphne was born, I started preparing the vegetables during naptime so I only had to stir everything together before we wanted to eat. It is so convenient to have the prep work out of the way when everyone is hungry.

naptime stopwatch

10 minutes prep time
25 minutes cook time

makes 4 servings

1 pound asparagus

5 tablespoons unsalted butter, divided

1 medium yellow onion, finely chopped

1 $\frac{1}{2}$ cups Arborio rice

$\frac{1}{2}$ cup dry white wine

4 cups low-sodium chicken stock

$\frac{1}{2}$ cup (2 ounces) freshly grated Parmesan cheese

1 teaspoon kosher salt

Pinch freshly ground black pepper

1. Trim the asparagus by snapping off the tough bottom of each stalk where it naturally breaks when bent. Bring a wide pot of water to a boil over medium heat, add the trimmed asparagus, and cook it until it is tender enough to be pierced with a fork, about 3 to 5 minutes. Drain the water and cut the asparagus into 2-inch pieces. Set aside.

2. In a low, wide sauté pan, heat 4 tablespoons of the butter over medium heat. Allow the butter to warm until it is bubbly, turns a golden brown, and has a nutty fragrance, about 2 to 3 minutes. Keep swirling the butter around the pan as it cooks so the milk solids don't burn.

3. Add the chopped onion to the pan and sauté it in the brown butter until it is translucent and tender, about 4 to 5 minutes.

4. Stir the rice into the pan. Carefully pour in the wine, scrape up any browned bits from the bottom of the pan with a wooden spoon, and simmer the wine until it has reduced by half.

5. Pour $\frac{1}{2}$ cup of the chicken stock into the pan and stir it continuously with the rice until it has been completely absorbed, about 3 minutes. Repeat this procedure, adding chicken stock to the rice by the $\frac{1}{2}$ cup until all of the chicken stock has been absorbed. This will take some time so be patient: Monitor it closely and don't leave the stove.

6. Once all the chicken stock has been added and the risotto has softened and is tender to the bite, remove it from the heat and stir in the Parmesan cheese and remaining 1 tablespoon of butter. Taste the risotto and add a pinch or two of salt if necessary.

7. Finally, using a wooden spoon, stir the asparagus pieces into the risotto and finish off with a few grinds of black pepper. Serve hot.

variation ideas: The rich, nutty taste of browned butter stands up well to a variety of vegetables, especially mushrooms or butternut squash. Either are excellent substitutes for the cooked asparagus spears. For mushrooms, sauté the slices in a skillet with a touch of olive oil and stir them into the risotto as directed in Step 7. For butternut squash, add 2 cups of squash diced into $\frac{1}{4}$-inch cubes at the same time you add the onion in Step 3. Then follow the remaining steps as written above.

spicy sausage-stuffed shells

Stuffed shells are often viewed as kids' food, but I beg to differ. I like to stuff them with a hearty scoop of sausage and fresh cheese and then cover them with a rich homemade sauce. I assemble the whole dish during the day and then bake it when we're ready to eat. Jumbo size shells can vary depending on the brand of pasta; the shells I buy are about 3 inches long. If you buy bigger shells, adjust the proportions by stuffing fewer shells, with more of the filling and nestle them in the same size baking dish as instructed below.

naptime stopwatch

25 minutes prep time
35 minutes bake time

makes 6 to 8 servings

12 ounces jumbo-sized shells (about 25 shells)

3 teaspoons olive oil, divided

3 garlic cloves, minced and divided

1 (28-ounce) can crushed tomatoes, with juices

1 cup (8 ounces) fresh ricotta cheese

½ cup (4 ounces) full-fat cottage cheese

¾ cup (5 ounces) shredded mozzarella

⅔ cup (3 ounces) freshly grated Parmesan cheese, divided

1 large egg, lightly beaten

¼ cup finely chopped fresh parsley

(continued)

1. Preheat the oven to 350°F.

2. Cook the pasta shells according to package instructions, drain well, and set aside.

3. In a large saucepan, warm 1 teaspoon of olive oil over medium heat. Add 2 of the minced garlic cloves and sauté for about 2 minutes, or until the garlic becomes fragrant. Carefully add the tomatoes and sauté them over medium-low heat for about 15 minutes, or until the sauce thickens.

4. While the sauce is simmering, mix together the ricotta, cottage cheese, mozzarella, ⅓ cup of the Parmesan, egg, parsley, basil, crushed red pepper, and salt in a large bowl and set aside.

5. In a large skillet over medium-high heat, add the remaining 2 teaspoons of olive oil, the sausage, and the remaining garlic, and sauté until the meat is cooked through and no longer pink. As the sausage cooks, break up any large chunks of meat with a wooden spoon. Add the red wine and scrape up any browned bits from the bottom of the skillet and allow the mixture to simmer until the wine has reduced by half. Carefully add three-quarters of the tomato sauce to the sausage, reserving the rest, and simmer on low heat for 5 minutes, stirring often. Once the mixture has thickened slightly, remove the pan from the heat.

6. Spread 1 or 2 tablespoons of the reserved tomato sauce in the bottom of a 13 x 9-inch baking dish. To prepare the shells, use a wide spoon to scoop about 1 tablespoon of the sausage sauce and 1 tablespoon of the cheese mixture into each pasta shell. Arrange the shells snugly in the baking dish, seam-side down.

7. When all the shells are filled, pour the remaining tomato sauce evenly over the shells so that they are completely covered and sprinkle with remaining ⅓ cup of Parmesan.

8. Bake the shells for 35 to 40 minutes, or until the mixture is hot and bubbly. If the top begins to brown too quickly, cover the dish loosely with aluminum foil.

make-ahead tips: Assemble the whole dish at naptime and chill, covered, before baking, or save time by assembling the sausage sauce in advance.

2 tablespoons finely chopped fresh basil

½ teaspoon crushed red pepper flakes

½ teaspoon kosher salt

1 pound spicy Italian sausage, casings removed

¼ cup dry red wine

meatballs for choir boys

My grandmother Pat, an excellent cook, hosted a spaghetti-and-meatball dinner for my father's church choir every Friday night when he was young. At the top of the recipe card for her famous meatballs she noted, "Have made at least a trillion!" I don't think that was inaccurate: These meatballs fed a lot of hungry boys! Our family still adores these to this day. Daphne loves them so much I can barely keep the freezer stocked!

naptime stopwatch

20 minutes prep time
25 minutes cook time

makes about 24 to 28 medium-sized meatballs

2 slices white bread

½ cup whole milk

⅓ pound ground beef (85% lean)

⅓ pound ground pork

⅓ pound ground veal

½ cup (2 ounces) freshly grated Parmesan cheese

2 large eggs, lightly beaten

1 garlic clove, minced

2 teaspoons finely chopped fresh parsley

1 teaspoon kosher salt

¼ teaspoon freshly ground black pepper

2 teaspoons vegetable oil, plus more as needed

1. Preheat the oven to 400°F.

2. Place the bread in a small bowl and pour the milk over it. Allow the bread to soak for 2 minutes, or until all of the milk is absorbed. Tear the bread into very small chunks and leave it in the bowl.

3. Combine all the meats in a large bowl and form a little well in the middle. Add the cheese, eggs, garlic, parsley, salt, pepper, and bread chunks in the well and use clean hands or a wooden spoon to combine all of the ingredients by folding and refolding the meat. Check to see that everything is evenly distributed then stop working the meat; it should still be a little loose.

4. Set a foil-lined rimmed baking sheet next to your bowl. Pinch off pieces of the meat and form meatballs that are 1½ inches in diameter (about a tablespoon and a half). Do not compact the meat too much; roll the meat lightly so that there are still small pockets of air. Place the meatballs on the lined baking sheet.

5. Warm the oil in large wide skillet over medium-high heat. Cook the meatballs in batches, turning them slightly with a spatula (do not use tongs—they will break the delicate meatballs) for 5 minutes to make sure all sides are browned. This sears the meat and keeps the flavorful juices inside when they bake in the oven. Add an additional tablespoon of oil if needed to sear remaining batches.

6. Replace the foil on the baking sheet with a new sheet. Place the meatballs 1 inch apart on the baking sheet and place in the oven. Bake for 20 to 22 minutes or until cooked through. Serve hot.

Opposite page, clockwise from top: The Best Garlic Bread, page 146; Spicy Sausage-Stuffed Shells, page 112; Meatballs for Choir Boys, this page

make-ahead tips: These meatballs freeze beautifully. To freeze, allow them to cool completely after baking. Slide the meatballs on the baking sheet into the freezer for 2 hours. Then place the frozen meatballs in a freezer bag, folding it over to remove any air before sealing. To reheat, place the frozen meatballs on a rimmed baking sheet in an oven preheated to 350°F for 20 to 25 minutes or until they are completely warmed through.

variation ideas: If there is no veal or pork available, these can be made with all beef. These meatballs are terrific with dishes besides spaghetti: Serve them in broth to make a meatball soup or on a sub roll with marinara sauce and grated cheese.

three-cheese turkey lasagna

This is a hearty, stick-to-your-ribs lasagna. Making it ahead is easy; it can be completely assembled and chilled up to a day before you intend to bake it. Paired with a Tri-Color Salad with Parmesan & Pine Nuts (page 61) and The Best Garlic Bread (page 148), it is the perfect meal for cozy nights at home.

naptime
stopwatch

30 minutes prep time
1 hour cook time

makes 8 to 10 servings

Unsalted butter, as needed

2 teaspoons olive oil

1 medium yellow onion,
finely chopped

2 garlic cloves, minced

1 pound ground turkey

42 ounces crushed tomatoes,
with juices (from one 14-ounce
can and one 28-ounce can)

¼ cup coarsely chopped
fresh basil

1 teaspoon kosher salt

½ teaspoon freshly ground
black pepper

2 cups (1 pound) fresh ricotta
cheese

3 large eggs

1 (10-ounce) bag frozen
chopped spinach, thawed
and drained

1 pinch crushed red pepper
flakes

(continued)

1. Preheat the oven to 350°F. Lightly butter a deep 13 x 9-inch baking dish and set aside.

2. Heat the olive oil in a large pot over medium heat. Add the onion and cook until it is completely translucent, about 3 to 5 minutes. Add the garlic and cook everything for 1 more minute, or until the garlic is fragrant. Increase the heat to medium-high and add the ground turkey. Cook the meat until it is no longer pink, breaking it apart with a wooden spoon as it cooks.

3. Once the meat is cooked through, carefully add the crushed tomatoes, basil, salt, and pepper to the turkey mixture and allow everything to simmer on low heat for 10 minutes, or until it has slightly thickened.

4. While the tomato sauce is simmering, combine the ricotta, egg, spinach, red pepper flakes, and nutmeg in a large bowl and set aside.

5. To assemble the lasagna, ladle a small amount of the tomato sauce in the bottom of the prepared baking dish so that it is evenly covered. Layer 4 of the no-bake noodles, or 3 of the regular noodles, in the bottom of the pan. On top of the noodles spread one-half of the ricotta mixture followed by one-third of the sauce. On top of the sauce sprinkle one-third of the shredded mozzarella and one-third of the Parmesan. Add a layer of the noodles on top of the cheese and repeat this process to make the second layer.

6. Place the remaining noodles on top of the lasagna and spread the remaining one-third of the sauce on top, along with the remaining one-third of the mozzarella and Parmesan.

7. Place the baking dish on a baking sheet and cover it with aluminum foil. Bake the lasagna for 50 minutes, or until the sauce is bubbly and the cheese is melted. Remove the foil and bake the lasagna for another 5 to 10 minutes, or until the top of the lasagna is golden brown. When it is done, allow the lasagna to cool on the counter and firm up for 10 minutes. Serve warm.

make-ahead tips: It is perfectly fine to make this with store-bought tomato sauce. Or you can make the homemade tomato sauce several days in advance; it will keep in the refrigerator for a week or more. The lasagna can easily be assembled and stored in the refrigerator for up to a day before baking it. Alternatively, bake it ahead of time and simply reheat it for dinner.

variation ideas: If you substitute ground beef for the turkey, be sure to drain off the grease before adding the tomato sauce.

½ teaspoon freshly grated nutmeg

1 (12-ounce) box no-bake lasagna noodles (substitute regular lasagna noodles, cooked according to package directions)

8 ounces fresh mozzarella, shredded

1 cup (4 ounces) freshly grated Parmesan cheese

amazing shrimp scampi

It took me a long time to come around to shrimp. Growing up in Cooperstown, a small town in upstate New York, the selection of fresh seafood was slim, and the only shrimp I knew of were frozen. When I finally had my first taste of the fresh variety, I was hooked and started cooking it regularly. This decadent dish dresses up the everyday shrimp with a fragrant herbaceous butter sauce. If you ever need to introduce someone to shrimp, this is a great place to start!

naptime stopwatch

10 minutes prep time
20 minutes cook time

makes 4 servings

1 pound small shrimp, shelled and deveined

1 pound linguine or any long pasta

½ cup olive oil

2 garlic cloves, minced

10 ounces (2½ sticks) unsalted butter, cubed

1½ teaspoons dried basil

1 teaspoon dried oregano

1 teaspoon finely chopped fresh parsley

2 tablespoons dry white wine

Zest and juice of 1 medium lemon

1½ teaspoons kosher salt

¼ teaspoon freshly ground black pepper

1. Preheat the oven to 450°F.

2. In a shallow baking dish, arrange the shrimp in one even layer and set aside.

3. Bring a large stockpot of salted water to a boil and cook the pasta according to package directions until al dente. Drain the pasta and set aside.

4. While the pasta is cooking, warm the olive oil in a saucepan over medium heat. Add the minced garlic and simmer gently in the olive oil until the garlic is softened and fragrant, about 1 minute. Shake the pan gently a bit so that the garlic doesn't burn in the oil.

5. Add the butter, basil, oregano, parsley, wine, lemon juice, lemon zest, salt, and pepper to the pan. Allow the butter to melt, and cook the sauce for 3 minutes, allowing the flavors to blend.

6. Pour approximately half of the sauce over the shrimp and toss to coat the baking dish and the shrimp. Reserve the remaining sauce for the pasta. Place the shrimp in the oven and bake for 5 minutes or until they are a light pink color.

7. Divide the hot pasta evenly among 4 serving bowls and toss each bowl with ½ cup of the hot butter sauce. Place about 8 of the hot shrimp on top of the pasta in each bowl and serve. Save any remaining butter sauce in a sealed container in the fridge.

make-ahead tips: The shrimp and sauce can easily be prepared in advance. Make the sauce and allow it to cool to room temperature. Then prepare the shrimp in the pan (do not bake) and add the cooled sauce as directed in Step 6. Cover the dish with plastic wrap and chill it in the refrigerator until ready to cook. It will hold like this for up to a day. Store the remaining butter sauce in a plastic container and reheat it on the stovetop before tossing with freshly cooked pasta.

serving ideas: Crusty bread is a must with this dish. Use it to mop up all of the delicious buttery sauce at the bottom of the bowl. When serving this to children, don't forget the bibs.

spicy citrus grilled shrimp

This fun, easy dish has a summery feel to it when grilled on skewers and eaten al fresco. The shrimp can easily be prepared at any time during the day and grilled up in no time for dinner.

 naptime
stopwatch

15 minutes prep time
5 minutes cook time

makes 4 servings

20 large shrimp, shelled and deveined with tails left on

¾ cup olive oil

¼ cup freshly squeezed lemon juice

6 garlic cloves, minced

½ teaspoon cayenne pepper

½ teaspoon kosher salt

1. Prepare 4 skewers: If using wooden skewers, be sure to soak them in water for 5 minutes before adding the shrimp so that they do not burn on the grill. Place 5 shrimp on each skewer so that they are just touching, but not too close together.

2. In a small bowl, whisk together the olive oil, lemon juice, minced garlic, cayenne pepper, and salt. Pour the mixture into a large plastic freezer bag (1 gallon size) and add the shrimp skewers. Swish the mixture around the shrimp in the bag so that they are totally covered. Seal and place the bag inside a second bag or on a dish in the refrigerator and marinate the shrimp for at least 4 hours.

3. Heat the grill or a stovetop grill pan to medium heat and add the marinated shrimp skewers. Grill the skewers for about 3 minutes per side, or until the shrimp are pink and cooked through.

make-ahead tips: This recipe doubles or triples easily. If making a large batch, pour the marinade into a large baking dish and submerge the shrimp to marinate on the skewers. Then cover it with plastic and refrigerate them until right before grilling.

serving ideas: For a fun summer meal, serve these with Soba Noodle Salad (page 58), Real Tex-Mex Guacamole (page 50), and Strawberry Margaritas (page 200).

roast salmon with herbed crème fraîche

I've always loved roasting salmon with mayonnaise or crème fraîche because it produces such a moist and flaky fish. One day when I had a glut of fresh herbs from my garden I added them to the crème fraîche for extra flavor. We loved how the delicate herb flavors infused the sweet salmon, and I've been preparing it this way ever since.

naptime stopwatch

5 minutes prep time
15 minutes cook time

makes 6 to 8 servings

2 pounds salmon, cut into 4 portions

⅓ cup crème fraîche

5 leaves fresh basil

2 teaspoons fresh parsley

2 teaspoons fresh dill

2 teaspoons fresh thyme leaves

Kosher salt and freshly ground black pepper

1. Preheat the oven to 425°F and line a baking sheet with a double layer of aluminum foil.

2. In a food processor fitted with the blade attachment add the crème fraîche, basil, parsley, dill, thyme, and a pinch of salt and pepper. Process the crème until smooth and the herbs are completely incorporated.

3. Place the salmon on the baking sheet skin-side down and spread the herbed crème fraîche evenly on top of the fish.

4. Bake the salmon for 14 to 16 minutes, or until it is just cooked through and opaque in the center. Allow the salmon to cool for 5 minutes before serving.

make-ahead tips: Make the herbed crème fraîche ahead of time and keep it in the refrigerator before using.

variation ideas: The crème fraîche makes a decadent sauce when twirled into freshly cooked pasta, an ideal easy, quick meal.

poached salmon with leeks

My mother-in-law made this for me one of the first times I visited her house. I instantly loved the simplicity of the flavors, the soft, oniony leeks against the flaky poached fish. She gave me the recipe and it was added to our weeknight repertoire. I often pair this with Couscous with Tomato and Arugula (page 59) when we are in the mood for an easy, light dinner. I've also doubled or tripled the recipe for casual dinner parties.

naptime stopwatch

10 minutes prep time
20 minutes cook time

makes 4 servings

8 medium leeks

1 tablespoon unsalted butter

2½ cups chicken stock, plus more as needed

4 (6- to 8-ounce) salmon steaks, skin removed

1 teaspoon kosher salt

1 teaspoon freshly ground black pepper

1. Trim off the roots and dark green leaves of the leeks, leaving the soft white and light green parts. Slice each leek in half lengthwise. Then, slice each half into 1-inch half-moon shapes and place them in a bowl of lukewarm water. Use your fingers to swish the leeks around in the water vigorously, loosening the dirt caught within the layers. Let the leeks sit for 5 minutes. Scoop the leeks out of the dirty water, drain the bowl and refill it with clean water. Repeat the leek rinsing process again until the water remains clean. Place the clean leeks on a clean kitchen towel and thoroughly pat them dry.

2. Melt the butter in a large sauté pan over medium heat. Swirl the pan so that the butter covers the bottom entirely. Increase the heat to medium-high, add the leeks to the warm butter, and sauté until they are tender and slightly translucent, about 10 minutes.

3. Slowly pour in the chicken stock until it just covers the leeks. If you need a little more stock then the 1½ cups called for, add more in ¼ cup increments. Place the salmon steaks on top, making sure they are not touching. Sprinkle the steaks with salt and pepper.

4. Bring the stock to a light simmer. Place the lid on the pan and cook the salmon for 8 minutes. After that, check the salmon for doneness by flaking a small piece of the top with a fork. If the salmon is still raw inside, continue poaching for 1 to 2 more minutes, keeping a close eye on the fish.

5. Divide the leeks among 4 plates. Serve one salmon steak on top of each bed of leeks.

make-ahead: This simple meal can be prepared even more quickly if the leeks are chopped and rinsed prior to cooking. I often rinse and dry my leeks earlier in the day.

variation ideas: Instead of salmon, try this method with halibut or cod. Both taste wonderful with the oniony leeks.

pesto goat cheese-stuffed chicken breasts

This is one of those dinners that seems incredibly sophisticated and only takes a few minutes to prepare. The chicken can be stuffed during naptime and refrigerated for the afternoon, or prepared from scratch in the evening. The tangy pesto goat cheese is the perfect topping for a moist chicken breast, giving it terrific flavor without being too heavy.

naptime stopwatch

10 minutes prep time
40 minutes cook time

makes 4 servings

1 (8-ounce) log plain goat cheese, at room temperature

3 tablespoons fresh pesto (homemade page 204, or store-bought)

4 split bone-in, skin-on chicken breasts (about 1 ¾ to 2 pounds)

¼ cup olive oil

Kosher salt and freshly ground black pepper

1. Preheat the oven to 375°F. Line a baking sheet with aluminum foil.

2. In a mixing bowl, stir together the goat cheese and pesto until evenly incorporated.

3. Carefully pull back the skin on the top of each chicken breast so that a pocket forms. Stuff 2 ounces of the pesto goat cheese (one-quarter of the mixture) into the pocket, smoothing it into an even layer. Then pull the skin back over the chicken to cover as much of the cheese and meat as possible.

4. Rub each chicken breast all over with the olive oil and sprinkle the tops with a pinch of salt and black pepper and place them bone-side down on the prepared baking sheet. Bake the chicken, uncovered, for 40 to 45 minutes, or until the breasts are cooked through and the skin is golden and crispy.

make-ahead tips: The chicken can be stuffed at any point during the day and stored in the refrigerator before baking. I recommend doing this because refrigerating the stuffed chicken for an hour or two will make the meat especially moist and flavorful. If you don't have time to stuff the chicken ahead of time, stir together the pesto and goat cheese and it will last covered in the refrigerator for several days. Then it will always be ready whenever you have to get the chicken in the oven quickly.

serving ideas: To round out this simple, hearty meal serve it with a Tri-Color Salad with Parmesan & Pine Nuts (page 161) and Creamy Parmesan & Chive Polenta (page 73).

teriyaki baked chicken thighs

This is one of the first dishes I started cooking during naptime when Daphne was an infant. It is so simple that I could easily prepare it during the day, no matter how sleep-deprived I was. I still make it on days when I have very little time to cook—just 5 minutes is all it takes to guarantee a great dinner when I need it most!

naptime
stopwatch

5 minutes prep time
55 minutes cook time

makes 8 to 10 servings

8 to 10 bone-in, skin-on chicken thighs (about 3 pounds)

1 ½ cups (10 ounces) teriyaki marinade

½ cup (4 ounces) soy sauce

2 tablespoons sesame seeds

1 cup chopped scallions (about 6), white and light green parts only

1. Preheat the oven to 350°F.

2. Place the chicken thighs skin-side up in a 13 x 9-inch baking dish, nestling them snugly together as needed. Whisk together the teriyaki, soy sauce and sesame seeds. Pour the marinade over the chicken thighs, using a spatula to make sure it gets underneath the chicken and completely covers the skin of each thigh.

3. Bake the chicken for 50 to 55 minutes, or until it is cooked through and the marinade has thickened and formed a sticky glaze. Use tongs to transfer the chicken to a serving platter and spoon some of the remaining sauce from the pan over the chicken. Top the chicken with the chopped scallions and serve.

make-ahead tips: The chicken can be prepared up to 1 day ahead of time and kept in the refrigerator covered with plastic wrap. Sometimes I prepare the chicken in the morning instead of during naptime.

sticky orange drumsticks

Drumsticks are one of those things that appeal to the child in all of us. Daphne loves getting messy while she eats these, and we do, too. Be sure you allow for enough time to marinate the drumsticks—at least 3 hours.

naptime
stopwatch

15 minutes prep time
45 minutes cook time

makes 4 servings

3 tablespoons honey

Zest and juice of 1 large orange

2 tablespoons dark soy sauce

2 tablespoons light soy sauce

8 chicken drumsticks (about 2 pounds)

2 tablespoons sesame seeds

1. In a small bowl, whisk together the honey, orange zest and juice, dark soy sauce, and light soy sauce. Set the marinade aside.

2. Make 3 slashes about ¼-inch wide on the top of each drumstick to help them absorb the marinade, and fit the drumsticks snugly into a 13 x 9-inch baking dish. Pour the marinade into the dish, turning each drumstick around one full rotation to evenly coat it with the marinade. Cover the dish and refrigerate the drumsticks for at least 3 hours, or up to 1 day.

3. Preheat the oven to 350°F.

4. Line a baking sheet with aluminum foil and place the drumsticks on it, skin-side up. Sprinkle the sesame seeds over the drumsticks and bake them for 45 minutes, brushing them with the leftover marinade halfway through. Remove them from the oven and allow them to cool slightly. Serve warm.

make-ahead tips: I often prepare these in the morning since the chicken can stay refrigerated for up to a day before being baked.

parmesan panko chicken with balsamic tomatoes

Like most children, Daphne loves chicken fingers. But I didn't want to spend the rest of her childhood eating basic breaded chicken, so I amped up the flavor by adding Parmesan cheese and panko breadcrumbs and topping it all with some marinated tomatoes and arugula. What was once a child's meal became a sophisticated recipe for our whole family.

naptime stopwatch
20 minutes prep time
10 minutes cook time

makes 4 servings

1 pint cherry tomatoes, halved

¼ cup olive oil, divided

2 tablespoons balsamic vinegar

Kosher salt and freshly ground black pepper

4 skinless boneless chicken breasts

1 large egg

½ cup all-purpose flour

2 cups panko breadcrumbs

1 cup (4 ounces) freshly grated Parmesan cheese

1 tablespoon unsalted butter

4 ounces (about 4 cups) arugula

1. In a bowl, combine the tomatoes with 2 tablespoons of olive oil, the balsamic vinegar, and a pinch of kosher salt and pepper. Toss the tomatoes a few times so they are coated with the oil mixture and leave them to marinate.

2. Place a large sheet of plastic wrap on the kitchen counter and line up the chicken breasts on it. Place a second sheet of plastic wrap on top of the chicken breasts so that they are completely covered. Using a meat pounder or heavy rolling pin, pound the chicken breasts until they are ⅛-inch thick, or as close to that thinness as possible.

3. Crack the egg into a medium bowl and whisk it well. Then place 2 plates on the countertop; pour the flour onto the first plate, and pour the panko and Parmesan cheese onto the second. Mix the Parmesan cheese and panko together with a fork so that the ingredients are evenly incorporated.

4. Lightly season a chicken breast with salt and pepper and dredge it in the plate of flour, making sure it is evenly coated with a light layer of flour. Then, dip the breast in the bowl of egg and turn it over until it is completely moistened. Finally, place the breast on the plate of Parmesan and panko and press down lightly so that the crunchy coating adheres well to the chicken. Flip the breast over and repeat this so that the entire breast is completely coated with the crumb mixture. Repeat with the remaining chicken breasts.

5. In a large skillet, heat the remaining 2 tablespoons of olive oil and 1 tablespoon of butter over medium-high until they are lightly bubbling. Swirl the butter to completely coat the bottom of the pan, then add 2 of the chicken breasts and cook them for about 6 minutes per side, or until the breadcrumbs are browned and crispy and the chicken is cooked through. Place the chicken on a plate lined with a paper towel to drain. Repeat with the remaining 2 chicken breasts.

6. To serve, place each chicken breast on a plate. Top each breast with ¼ of the arugula and a scoop of the marinated tomatoes, so that the toppings are evenly divided among the plates.

rosemary-lemon roast chicken

This is one of the first things I learned how to make when I started cooking on my own in New York after college. It took a few phone calls home to Mom to get it right. Since then I've roasted chickens dozens of ways and have developed my own favorite techniques. I think the bird tastes best when coated in herbs and lemon and roasted until crispy and aromatic. My favorite trick is seasoning the chicken in the morning while Daphne eats breakfast and letting it rest all day. The flavors permeate the bird for a few hours so when it roasts it stays incredibly moist and flavorful. One of the best things about roast chicken is the leftovers. After eating the roast chicken the first night, strip the bird of any remaining meat and use it for sandwiches or to toss with pasta the next day. Use the carcass to make chicken stock (page 214) for the freezer!

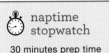

naptime stopwatch

30 minutes prep time
1 hour 30 minutes cook time

makes one 4- to
5-pound chicken

1 (4- to 5-pound) whole roaster chicken, giblets and neck removed

5 tablespoons fresh rosemary

Zest of 2 medium lemons

Juice of 1 medium lemon

3 tablespoons olive oil

1 tablespoon kosher salt

1 ½ teaspoons freshly ground black pepper

4 large garlic cloves

1. Rinse the chicken and pat it dry. Place the chicken on a rack in a roasting pan or in a large casserole dish.

2. Place the rosemary, lemon zest, lemon juice, olive oil, salt, pepper, and garlic cloves in a food processor fitted with a blade. Pulse until the mixture is completely combined and a loose paste forms.

3. Rub the entire chicken with the rosemary paste, including the top of the skin and underneath the skin, as well as inside the cavity of the bird. Quarter the second zested lemon that was not juiced and place it inside the cavity.

4. At this point the bird can be placed breast up in the pan, covered with plastic wrap, and refrigerated for up to 2 days.

5. Preheat the oven to 400°F. Remove the roasting pan from the refrigerator and let the chicken come to room temperature. Remove the plastic wrap, tuck the wing tips underneath the back, and roast the chicken for about 1 hour and 30 minutes. If the skin begins to brown too quickly toward the end of roasting, cover it lightly with foil. You'll know the chicken is done when the juices run clear and a meat thermometer inserted into the thickest part of the breast reads 180°F. Transfer the chicken to a carving board, cover it loosely with foil, and allow it to rest for 10 to 15 minutes before carving.

make-ahead tips: Preparing the chicken at least 3 hours before baking it is ideal. The advance preparation guarantees maximum flavor after cooking.

variation ideas: This paste tastes terrific with all kinds of herbs. Try adding oregano, basil, or thyme—or any combination of the three!

chicken curry

My friend Barbara makes the best curry. It is smooth and tangy and loaded up with all kinds of sweet and salty flavors. The most fun part about eating it is the toppings. Everyone chooses from dishes of shredded sweetened coconut, golden raisins, chopped peanuts and chopped scallions to sprinkle over their meal. When I asked Barbara how she gets this on the table on busy weeknights she explained that she cooks it when her kids are at school and reheats it on the stovetop right before dinner!

naptime
stopwatch

20 minutes prep time
45 minutes cook time

makes 6 to 8 servings

marinade

½ teaspoon curry powder

¼ teaspoon freshly ground black pepper

¼ teaspoon paprika

¼ cup honey

3 tablespoons Dijon mustard

2 tablespoons apricot jam

6 skinless boneless chicken breasts (about 2 to 2½ pounds)

2 cups uncooked jasmine rice

curry

2 tablespoons unsalted butter

2 medium yellow onions, finely chopped

4 garlic cloves, minced

(continued)

1. *To make the marinade:* In a small bowl, stir together the curry powder, black pepper, and paprika and set aside. In a separate bowl, stir together the honey, mustard, and apricot jam and set aside. Place the chicken breasts in a baking dish and sprinkle them evenly with the curry powder mixture. Then pour the apricot jam mixture over the chicken breasts and spread it around evenly to coat each breast. Cover the dish with plastic wrap and allow it to marinate in the refrigerator for at least 1 hour.

2. Preheat the oven to 350°F. Bake the chicken for about 40 to 45 minutes, or until it is cooked through and tender.

3. While the chicken is baking, prepare the jasmine rice according to package directions. When it is cooked, fluff it with a fork, cover the pan to keep warm, and set aside.

4. Allow the chicken to cool until it is comfortable enough to touch. Then use a fork to shred it into bite-sized pieces. Place the shredded chicken in a large mixing bowl and pour in any of the remaining liquid from the baking dish.

5. *To make the curry:* In a heavy large pot or Dutch oven, melt the butter over medium heat. Add the onions, garlic, and ginger and sauté until the onions are soft and translucent, about 5 minutes. Stir in the flour, curry powder, cinnamon, chili powder, turmeric, and cumin and cook for 1 more minute or until the mixture is fragrant.

6. Carefully pour the chicken stock into the pot, whisking continuously so that the onion and spices are completely incorporated into the stock. Add the yogurt, orange zest, and orange juice, stirring well so that the mixture thickens slightly and becomes smooth and creamy.

7. Add the shredded chicken to the pot and cook until the chicken is heated through. Do not bring the mixture to a boil or the yogurt will curdle. Spoon the curry onto plates over jasmine rice and sprinkle with coconut, raisins, peanuts, and scallions.

make-ahead tips: This entire dish can be made in advance and reheated gently on the stovetop for dinner.

1 tablespoon (from a 1-inch piece) chopped fresh ginger

2 tablespoons all-purpose flour

2 teaspoons curry powder

1 teaspoon ground cinnamon

1 teaspoon chili powder

1 pinch turmeric

1 pinch ground cumin

3 1/2 cups (28 ounces) low-sodium chicken stock

1 cup full-fat Greek yogurt

Zest and juice of 1 medium orange

1 cup shredded sweetened coconut, for serving

1 cup golden raisins, for serving

1 cup chopped roasted peanuts, for serving

1 bunch chopped scallions (1 cup), for serving

apricot-mustard glazed ham

This ham is one of our favorite special occasion meals. I always get accolades for the recipe and I never tell anyone that the topping only requires 3 ingredients. I drizzle the ham with this sweet glaze and put it in the oven. That is all there is to it!

naptime stopwatch

5 minutes prep time
1 hour 15 minutes
cook time

makes 1 (15-pound) ham

1 (15-pound) fully cooked spiral-cut ham

1 cup apricot jam

½ cup Dijon mustard

½ cup packed light brown sugar

1. Preheat the oven to 350°F.

2. In a small bowl, stir together the jam, mustard, and light brown sugar.

3. Place the ham in a roasting pan and brush the apricot-mustard glaze evenly over the ham. Bake for 1 hour and 15 minutes, or until the ham is heated through and the glaze is brown and bubbly. Remove the ham from the oven and tent it with aluminum foil for 10 minutes to rest. Slice and serve.

make-ahead tips: Making the glaze ahead of time is so simple. Simply brush it over the ham right before popping it in the oven.

serving ideas: One of the benefits of large hams is the leftovers. Enjoy them the next day on a hot open-faced sandwich.

variation ideas: If apricot jam is unavailable, orange jam or marmalade works well, too.

Opposite page, clockwise from top: Apricot-Mustard Glazed Ham, this page; Maple-Roasted Acorn Squash with Parmesan-Panko Topping, page 80; Roasted Potatoes with Herbed Salt, page 81

dutch oven pulled pork

This recipe was a huge hit on the blog the minute I posted it. Everyone still comments on the recipe's simplicity and terrific flavor. Preparing the pork during naptime takes all of 15 minutes. Then, after 3 hours of completely ignoring it as it cooks, dinner is ready to be shredded and served!

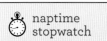
naptime stopwatch

15 minutes prep time
3 hours cook time

makes 6 to 8 servings

2 tablespoons vegetable oil

2 pounds boneless pork shoulder

½ medium yellow onion, finely chopped

½ cup crushed tomatoes, with juices

2 tablespoons tomato paste

¼ cup packed light brown sugar

1 tablespoon cayenne pepper

1 teaspoon crushed red pepper flakes

2 tablespoons Worcestershire sauce

¼ cup red wine vinegar

1 teaspoon kosher salt

1 teaspoon freshly ground black pepper

1. Preheat the oven to 325°F.

2. In a Dutch oven, heat the oil over medium heat until just smoking. Add the pork roast to the pot and sear all sides of the pork, including the ends. This will take about 1 to 2 minutes per side. Remove from the heat.

3. In a mixing bowl, whisk together the onion, tomatoes, tomato paste, sugar, cayenne, red pepper flakes, Worcestershire sauce, red wine vinegar, salt, and pepper until everything is completely combined. Carefully pour this mixture over the pork, turning the meat so that it is completely coated.

4. Place the lid on the Dutch oven and place it on the middle rack in the preheated oven. Braise the meat for 3 to 3½ hours, or until the pork is tender enough to be easily speared through with a knife and is no longer pink inside.

5. Remove the pot from the oven and remove the lid. Allow the pork to cool for 10 minutes in the pot. Transfer the meat to a cutting board and use 2 forks to shred it into bite-sized pieces. Once it is completely shredded, serve it with the remaining juices from the pot.

make-ahead tips: This recipe also works well in a slow cooker. Sear the pork as instructed above, transfer it to a slow-cooker, and cook it on low heat for at least 4 hours.

serving ideas: I am partial to pulled pork in soft tacos, tucked into corn tortillas and topped with sour cream, but this is also fabulous served on a soft roll and topped with caramelized onions.

perfect beef tenderloin

I used to be intimidated by the idea of cooking tenderloin until I discovered this no-fail cooking method. It yields a perfectly done beef tenderloin every time.

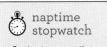

naptime stopwatch

5 minutes prep time
55 minutes cook time

makes 6 to 8 servings

1 (5- to 6-pound) beef tenderloin

Kosher salt and freshly ground black pepper

1. Remove the tenderloin from the refrigerator 2 hours before cooking and allow it to rest in a cool, dry place.

2. Preheat the oven to 425°F.

3. Place the tenderloin on a rack in a roasting pan and cover the roast generously with salt and pepper. Transfer to the oven and roast, uncovered, until it reaches desired doneness. For medium-rare, cook to an internal temperature of 130°F, about 30 to 35 minutes. For medium, cook to an internal temperature of 145°F, about 40 to 45 minutes.

4. Remove the pan from the oven. Cover the tenderloin loosely with a tent of aluminum foil and let it rest undisturbed for 20 minutes. (The temperature will continue to rise as the tenderloin rests.) Slice thinly and serve.

make-ahead tips: The tenderloin can be cooked ahead of time and stored in the refrigerator. To reheat, pre-heat the oven to 250°F degrees and warm it for 10 to 15 minutes.

serving ideas: This is great main course for a holiday meal. Pair it with Tri-Color Salad with Parmesan & Pine Nuts (page 61), Asparagus with Feta Vinaigrette (page 70), and Brussels Sprouts with Bacon & Cranberries (page 87) for a special family feast!

uncle will's killer burgers

My brother, known to Daphne as Uncle Will, is an amazing grill master. He dedicated many hours in college to perfecting his burger recipe, and it is our family favorite to this day. The spice powders and hot sauce create an intensely flavored patty that holds up well to the charcoal smoke. He also convinced me that incorporating the cheese into the beef is better than just melting it on top: The patty stays tender with flakes of melted cheese in each bite. For the finishing touch, Will swears that toasted potato buns are the way to go and, as with everything else about this recipe, I have to agree.

naptime stopwatch

10 minutes prep time
10 minutes cook time

makes 8 large burgers

3 pounds ground round (85% lean)

3 tablespoons of your favorite hot sauce (we like Cholula Hot Sauce)

3 tablespoons Worcestershire sauce

3 teaspoons garlic powder

3 teaspoons onion powder

1 teaspoon kosher salt

½ teaspoon freshly cracked black pepper

1 cup (4 ounces) coarsely grated sharp Cheddar cheese

8 potato hamburger buns, lightly toasted

Lettuce, for serving

Sliced onion, for serving

Ketchup, for serving

1. Preheat the grill to medium heat.

2. In a large bowl, combine the ground beef, hot sauce, Worcestershire sauce, garlic powder, onion powder, salt, pepper, and Cheddar cheese. Mix everything well with your hands until the ingredients are fully combined.

3. Form 8 equal-sized burger patties and grill the burgers over medium heat until cooked to desired doneness, about 10 to 15 minutes for medium doneness. For a medium-rare burger, grill for 8 to 10 minutes, or 15 to 18 minutes for well-done.

4. Serve each burger on a potato bun with lettuce, sliced onions, and a dollop of ketchup.

make-ahead tips: Burger patties can be formed in advance and frozen. To freeze them, wrap them individually in two layers of plastic wrap and an outer layer of aluminum foil. Formed patties will also last on a covered plate in the refrigerator for up to a day before grilling.

variation ideas: For a more decadent cheese, substitute Gorgonzola or Gruyère for the sharp Cheddar. Brioche buns or toasted sesame buns are good stand-ins if potato buns aren't available.

bistro steak with gorgonzola sauce

Duncan and I love a good steak dinner. To create our own steakhouse-style dinner at home, I prepare a rich Gorgonzola sauce and season the meat in advance. When he gets home from work, I simply light the grill and dinner is on the table in minutes.

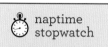

naptime stopwatch

20 minutes prep time
20 minutes cook time

makes 2 servings

steak

1 pound sirloin strip steak (about 1 ½-inches thick)

Kosher salt and freshly ground black pepper

¼ cup Worcestershire sauce, divided

sauce

2 tablespoons Gorgonzola cheese, crumbled

¼ cup mayonnaise

¼ cup full-fat sour cream

1 tablespoon heavy cream

1 teaspoon freshly ground black pepper

1. *To make the steak:* Sprinkle both sides of the steak liberally with salt, pepper, and 3 tablespoons of Worcestershire sauce. Light a grill and bring to medium heat or warm a stovetop grill pan over medium heat.

2. *To make the sauce:* In a small bowl, combine the Gorgonzola, mayonnaise, sour cream, heavy cream, pepper and remaining tablespoon Worcestershire sauce. Whisk together with a fork until completely combined. If the mixture is too thin, add a little more cream by the teaspoonful until you reach desired consistency.

3. Place the steaks on the grill and sear for 5 minutes. Use tongs to shift the steak 45 degrees on the pan to create crisscross grill marks. Sear for another 5 minutes and then turn it over and repeat this on the second side. This will cook the steak to medium doneness. Adjust cooking time accordingly to your preference. Remove the steak from the heat and cover it with aluminum foil and allow it to rest for 5 minutes. Slice the meat to desired thickness for serving, drizzle it with Gorgonzola Sauce and serve.

make-ahead tips: The sauce will stay for up to three days in the fridge. If it thickens in the refrigerator, stir in 1 or 2 teaspoons of cream to loosen it up before serving.

variation ideas: The Gorgonzola Sauce can also be used as a condiment for other recipes. It is an excellent dip for Crispy Parmesan Potato Wedges (page 82) or a simple vegetable crudité.

serving ideas: Roasted Potatoes with Herbed Salt (page 81) are perfect alongside this steak.

italian-style meatloaf

There was no way I was going to give up this family favorite after Daphne was born; the trick is to prepare the loaf and refrigerate it earlier in the day. I like to make it with Italian flavorings like my mom did for us growing up. The mozzarella cheese stuffing, fresh basil, and marinara sauce make it taste like an inside-out meatball. To complete our meatloaf meal, I often pop potatoes in the oven to bake for 45 minutes to 1 hour alongside the meatloaf.

naptime
stopwatch

20 minutes prep time
1 hour 5 minutes cook time

makes 4 servings

1 ½ pounds meatball mix
(equal amounts ground beef,
ground pork, and ground veal)

⅓ cup marinara sauce,
homemade (page 211)
or store-bought

1 large egg

3 tablespoons Italian
breadcrumbs

2 teaspoons Worcestershire
sauce

2 teaspoons Italian seasoning

½ teaspoon kosher salt

½ teaspoon freshly ground
black pepper

3 tablespoons coarsely
shredded fresh mozzarella

⅓ cup coarsely chopped
fresh basil

1. Preheat the oven to 350°F. In a large mixing bowl, combine the ground meats, marinara sauce, egg, breadcrumbs, Worcestershire sauce, Italian seasoning, salt, and pepper and use a fork to mix everything until completely combined.

2. On a clean work surface, pound out the meat with your hands until it is about 1-inch thick. Then, scatter the shredded mozzarella and most of the basil leaves in a line in the center, leaving a 1-inch border at either end. Fold up the sides and ends of the meatloaf and pinch the meat to seal in the cheese. Form a loaf shape with your hands and scatter the remaining basil leaves on top.

3. Transfer the meatloaf to a roasting pan lined with aluminum foil (do not use the rack; set the meatloaf directly in the pan) or a rimmed cooking sheet. (Note: I prefer this method to baking it in a loaf pan because I think it cooks the outside more evenly, and the loaf develops a better crust.)

4. Bake the meatloaf for 45 to 50 minutes on the convection setting, if available, or bake for about 1 hour and 5 to 10 minutes in a regular oven. To check if the meat is done, cut into the meatloaf and make sure it isn't pink on the inside; the internal temperature should read 170°F, and the outside should have a nice crust. Serve hot, with a fresh baked potato on the side.

make-ahead tips: The meatloaf can be formed ahead of time and refrigerated, wrapped tightly in plastic, for up to a day before baking.

variation ideas: Meatloaf ingredients are flexible. For a richer flavor, substitute Gorgonzola for the mozzarella.

breads

buttermilk pecan banana bread

My mom's banana bread is the comfort food of my childhood. I still make it often and love to pack it for Daphne's preschool snack. People always swoon when they have a taste; I've handed out the recipe dozens of times.

naptime stopwatch

15 minutes prep time
1 hour bake time

makes 1 loaf

6 tablespoons unsalted butter, plus more as needed for the pan

⅓ cup cultured buttermilk

2 large eggs

1 teaspoon vanilla extract

1 cup granulated sugar

3 ripe bananas, mashed with a fork

2 cups plus 1 teaspoon all-purpose flour, divided

2 teaspoons baking powder

1 teaspoon baking soda

½ teaspoon ground nutmeg

¾ cup pecans, coarsely chopped

1. Preheat the oven to 350°F. Butter a 9 x 5-inch loaf pan and set aside.

2. Melt the butter and pour it into a large heatproof bowl to cool slightly. Add the buttermilk, eggs, and vanilla to the cooled butter and whisk everything together. Then, add the sugar and stir until it is smooth and creamy. Add the mashed bananas to the wet ingredients and stir; the mixture will be lumpy.

3. In a large bowl, combine the 2 cups flour, baking powder, baking soda, and nutmeg. Pour the banana mixture into the dry ingredients and stir until the batter forms. It will still be somewhat lumpy from the banana, just make sure the flour is no longer visible. Toss the chopped pecans with the remaining teaspoon of flour and fold them into the batter with a rubber spatula until just incorporated.

4. Pour the batter into the prepared loaf pan and bake it for about 50 minutes to 1 hour, or until a cake tester inserted in the center comes out clean.

make-ahead tips: This banana bread freezes beautifully. Wrap it in a double layer of plastic wrap and an outer layer of aluminum foil and it will keep in the freezer for up to 3 months.

variation ideas: For a sweet twist, substitute mini chocolate chips for the pecans and scatter some raw sugar over the batter before baking to make a nice crunchy topping.

lemon-thyme no-knead bread

Once I learned how to make no-knead bread from Jim Lahey's recipe printed in the *New York Times*, I didn't stop. It is easily the best way for busy parents to make fresh bread at home; you start the dough a day before you want to bake it to allow for a long, slow, hands-off rising time. If Daphne is awake while I am making the dough I get her involved. She loves to be in charge of folding the dough after it has risen.

naptime
stopwatch

20 minutes prep time
45 minutes bake time

makes 1 loaf

3 cups all-purpose flour, plus more as needed for dusting

¼ teaspoon active dry yeast

2 teaspoons finely chopped fresh thyme

2 teaspoons freshly grated lemon zest

1 ¾ teaspoons kosher salt

1 ½ cups lukewarm water

Olive oil, as needed

1. In a large bowl, combine the flour, yeast, thyme, lemon zest, and salt. Add the water and stir everything with a wooden spoon until all of the ingredients are blended and the dough begins to form into a ball. The dough will be very sticky. Cover the bowl with plastic wrap and let it sit at room temperature for 12 to 18 hours, or until the dough has almost doubled in size and the surface is dotted with small bubbles.

2. Remove the dough from the bowl and place it on a lightly floured cutting board. Sprinkle the dough with additional flour and fold it over itself twice. Sprinkle the top lightly with more flour and cover the dough loosely with plastic wrap and allow it to rest for 15 minutes.

3. Flour your hands and quickly shape the dough into a round loaf shape. Coat the cutting board very generously with flour and place the dough seam-side down on the board. Dust the top with flour and cover it with a clean kitchen towel. Allow the dough to rise until it has doubled in size and does not readily spring back when poked with a finger, about 2 hours.

4. Preheat the oven to 450°F and place an uncovered 2¾-quart cast-iron pot in the oven and allow it to warm for 30 minutes. Remove the pot from the oven and lightly brush the inside with olive oil. Gently transfer the bread dough from the cutting board and carefully place it in the hot greased pot. Place the pot in the oven with the lid on and bake it for 30 minutes. After 30 minutes, remove the cover and bake it for another 15 to 20 minutes, or until the loaf is evenly browned and the top is crusty. Remove the pot from the oven, place it on a wire rack and allow the bread to cool in the pot for 10 minutes. Carefully remove the loaf from the pot and allow it to cool completely on a rack before cutting and serving.

variation ideas: You can try many variations with this herb-infused bread. Rosemary, basil, or oregano are all excellent substitutes if thyme is unavailable.

the best garlic bread

The key to perfect garlic bread is garlic butter. I spread big swaths of it on fresh crusty bread and bake it to perfection. Everyone goes wild for its deep garlic flavor and buttery crunch.

naptime stopwatch

10 minutes prep time
10 minutes cook time

makes 1 loaf

4 ounces (1 stick) unsalted butter, at room temperature

8 garlic cloves, minced

2 tablespoons finely chopped fresh parsley

¼ teaspoon kosher salt

¾ cup (3 ounces) freshly grated Parmesan cheese

1 loaf good French bread

1. Preheat the oven to 375°F.

2. In a small bowl, stir together the softened butter, garlic, parsley, and salt.

3. Slice the bread in half lengthwise. Spread half of the garlic butter on each cut side of the bread.

4. Place the bread halves back together and wrap the loaf tightly in a single layer of aluminum foil. Bake the bread for 10 minutes.

5. Turn on the broiler. Reopen the bread and place the halves, cut-side up, on a baking sheet. Sprinkle the Parmesan cheese evenly over both halves of the bread and place the baking sheet under the broiler for 1 minute, or until the cheese turns a deep burnished brown color. Remove immediately, slice into pieces, and serve hot.

make-ahead tips: Make the garlic butter ahead of time so you can throw this bread together in a jiffy at dinner. I make garlic butter often and keep it in the refrigerator for a variety of things. It is excellent tossed with pasta or mussels.

variation ideas: For a twist, try using basil or thyme in the butter instead of parsley. Basil garlic butter can be melted to a make a fantastic sauce for gnocchi.

herbs de provence popovers

These are always wildly popular in our house. I added herbs de Provence to my regular popover recipe one day to give them a new twist. I love the soft herbal flavors mixed into the airy bread. Since I rarely buy kitchen equipment that serves only one purpose, I bake these in muffin tins instead of specialized popover tins. You can use a popover pan if you have one.

naptime stopwatch

10 minutes prep time
35 minutes bake time

makes 12 popovers

4 large eggs, at room temperature

1 cup all-purpose flour

1 pinch kosher salt

1 pinch freshly ground black pepper

½ cup heavy cream, at room temperature

1 cup whole milk, at room temperature

2 tablespoons unsalted butter, melted and cooled

3 tablespoons herbs de Provence

1. Preheat the oven to 400°F. Spray a 12-cup muffin tin with nonstick spray, or a 6-cup jumbo muffin tin, depending on the size you'd like the popovers to be.

2. In the bowl of an electric mixer fitted with a paddle attachment, slowly beat the eggs, flour, salt, and pepper until just blended.

3. Scrape down the sides of the bowl with a rubber spatula. With the mixer on low speed, add the cream, milk, and melted butter and mix until everything is smooth and completely incorporated. Stir in the herbs de Provence with a rubber spatula.

4. Divide the batter evenly among the muffin cups so that each cup is about two-thirds full. Bake the popovers for 35 minutes, or until they puff up and are a light golden brown. Do not open the oven door while the popovers are baking; this may cause them to fall prematurely. Allow the popovers to cool until just comfortable enough to touch. Or, if you want to save them for dinner, pierce a tiny hole in the tops so that they don't fall before serving them.

make-ahead tips: The batter can easily be made ahead of time and stored in the refrigerator in a jar or pitcher until you are ready to bake.

serving ideas: I serve these with a warm soup or Perfect Beef Tenderloin (page 135).

perfect every time cornbread

Duncan grew up eating this cornbread; the recipe is from his mother's best friend, Barb McChesney. He gave me this recipe early on in our courtship, and it has become a staple in our kitchen. It is easy to make ahead of time or at a moment's notice. The recipe is so versatile; it is fun to doctor up the batter with a little bit of this or that—see the variation suggestions, below, for ideas. You can easily tweak the flavor to pair it with whatever you are serving.

naptime stopwatch

10 minutes prep time
30 minutes bake time

makes one 9-inch square pan

Unsalted butter, as needed

¾ cup yellow cornmeal

¾ cup all-purpose flour

½ cup granulated sugar

1 ¼ teaspoons baking powder

1 teaspoon kosher salt

1 large egg

⅔ cup whole milk

1. Preheat the oven to 350°F. Butter a 9 x 9-inch baking pan, paying special attention to the corners, and set aside.

2. In a mixing bowl, combine the cornmeal, flour, sugar, baking powder, and salt, and whisk everything together. Crack the egg into the dry ingredients and stir well to combine. Pour in the milk and stir until the batter is smooth and creamy.

3. Pour the batter into the prepared baking pan and bake for 25 to 30 minutes, or until the edges are golden and slightly pulled away from the edge of the pan and the top springs back when touched.

make-ahead tips: This moist bread can be made up to a day before you want to serve it. Reheat it in the oven or microwave right before serving.

variation ideas: This recipe is an ideal backdrop for many flavors. For a savory twist, add 1 cup of grated sharp Cheddar cheese to the batter at the same time you add the egg. For extra heat, add ¼ cup seeded diced jalapeño peppers to the batter. During corn season, add kernels from a freshly cooked ear of corn.

chocolate zucchini loaf

This unlikely combination of vegetables and chocolate straddles the line between health food and dessert. The loaf rises to a beautifully crackly top and is as moist as a dense cake. I like to bake it in the afternoon so Daphne can have a warm slice for a snack when she wakes up. Sometimes we even have it for dessert in the summer with a scoop of ice cream.

naptime stopwatch

25 minutes prep time
80 minutes bake time

makes 1 loaf

Unsalted butter, as needed

3 large eggs, at room temperature

2 cups granulated sugar

1 cup vegetable oil

¼ cup full-fat yogurt, stirred well

3 teaspoons vanilla extract

2 cups freshly grated zucchini (1 medium-to-large zucchini)

3 cups all-purpose flour, plus more as needed for the pan

½ cup unsweetened cocoa powder, sifted

1 tablespoon ground cinnamon

1 teaspoon kosher salt

1 teaspoon baking soda

¼ teaspoon baking powder

1. Preheat the oven to 350°F. Butter and flour a 9 x 5-inch loaf pan and set aside.

2. In a large mixing bowl, whisk together the eggs, sugar, vegetable oil, yogurt, and vanilla until everything is incorporated. Mix in the grated zucchini and set aside.

3. In a separate bowl, combine the flour, cocoa powder, cinnamon, salt, baking soda, and baking powder and stir them together with a whisk.

4. Pour the dry ingredients into the wet ingredients and mix them well with a wooden spoon until the flour is no longer visible. Pour the batter into the prepared loaf pan and bake it for 1 hour and 15 minutes, or until the top of the loaf is set and springs back lightly when touched. Allow the bread to cool for 10 minutes in the pan before releasing it onto a wire rack. Then allow it to cool to room temperature before serving.

make-ahead tips: To freeze some for winter, wrap each loaf in a double layer of plastic wrap and an outer layer of aluminum foil. For an especially decadent treat, eat a slice straight from the freezer.

serving ideas: The loaf also transports well. It is great for potlucks or taking to new parents. Sometimes I pack a few slices in our beach bag for an afternoon seaside treat.

desserts

strawberry-rhubarb crunch
with frozen strawberry whipped cream

Rhubarb is one of my favorite summer vegetables. It grew in my parents' garden when I was a child and we ate it stewed with sugar and drizzled over ice cream all summer long. This fun pie combines the classic rhubarb-berry pairing with crunchy oatmeal and a fluffy frozen topping.

naptime stopwatch

30 minutes prep time
1 hour bake time

makes one 9-inch pie

2 ¼ cups (10 ounces) fresh strawberries, washed, hulled, and sliced

4 cups (1 pound) rhubarb, cut into 1-inch pieces, ends trimmed

¾ cup granulated sugar, divided

2 tablespoons cornstarch

1 ½ cups all-purpose flour

1 cup packed dark brown sugar

1 cup quick-cooking oats

1 teaspoon ground cinnamon

4 ounces (1 stick) unsalted butter, melted and cooled, plus more as needed for the pie plate

1 cup heavy whipping cream

1. Preheat the oven to 325°F. Butter a 9-inch pie plate and set aside.

2. Set aside ¼ cup of the strawberries for the topping.

3. In a large saucepan, combine the remaining strawberries, rhubarb, ½ cup sugar, and the cornstarch. Cook over low heat, stirring constantly, until the fruit has softened and thickened, about 10 minutes. Remove the pan from the heat and cover.

4. In a small bowl, combine the flour, brown sugar, oats, cinnamon, and melted butter. Work the mixture together with your fingertips or a wooden spoon until it forms a coarse crumb.

5. Press two-thirds of the oatmeal crunch evenly into the bottom of the prepared pie plate with your hands. Pour the warm cooked fruit on top of the crumb layer and sprinkle the remaining oatmeal crunch on top.

6. Bake the pie for 55 to 65 minutes, or until the mixture is warm and bubbly and the crunch topping is golden brown. Place the dish on a wire rack and cool to room temperature.

7. In an electric mixer fitted with the whisk attachment, whip the cream until it is thick, about 3 minutes. Add the remaining ¼ cup sugar and reserved ¼ cup strawberries to the cream and continue to beat the mixture until it is thick and glossy, about 3 more minutes.

8. Spread a large piece of waxed paper on the countertop and trace a 9-inch circle on it. Flip the waxed paper over so that the circle is on the other side and does not mark the topping. Spoon the whipped topping inside the outline of the circle and spread it evenly to form a circle shape. Freeze the topping on the waxed paper until it is firm, about 1 hour. Peel the waxed paper off and carefully place the topping on top of the cooled pie, and serve.

make-ahead tips: The flavor of this pie improves after it has cooled for a few hours. I recommend making it up to a day before you intend serve it. To speed up assembly, make the oatmeal crunch as instructed in Step 4 in advance and store it in the refrigerator for up to 3 days. Then you'll always have it on hand for this pie or any other crunchy dessert you wish to make.

serving ideas: The frozen topping makes this an especially refreshing dessert in the summer. To ramp up the visual effect, add a few drops of red food coloring to the cream while you're whipping it to give it a pretty pink hue. If you decide to skip the frozen cream, you can serve the pie with a scoop of ice cream instead.

classic summer peach pie

One of my first baking memories is of helping my mother make this pie. Working together, I rolled out the crust while she sliced the peaches. We made a dozen or so each summer. Half of the pies would be eaten right away and the other half would be frozen, unbaked, in the cellar freezer. Those were baked at Thanksgiving and Christmas when we hosted all of our friends and family for big holiday meals. The dough needs to chill for 2 hours, so plan ahead.

 naptime stopwatch

30 minutes prep time
50 minutes bake time

makes one 9-inch pie

pie crust

2 cups all-purpose flour, plus more as needed for dusting

½ teaspoon salt

6 ounces (1½ sticks) unsalted butter, chilled and cut into small pieces

¼ cup ice water

peach filling

2 pounds peaches, peeled, pitted, and sliced (4 cups), or 32 ounces frozen sliced peaches, thawed

¾ cup granulated sugar

1 teaspoon almond extract

Juice of ½ medium lemon (about 1 teaspoon)

2 tablespoons tapioca

1 large egg

1. *For the pie crust:* In a food processor fitted with a blade, combine the flour, salt, and butter. Pulse until a coarse meal forms, about 15 pulses. Add the ice water one tablespoon at a time, pulsing a few times after each addition, until the dough forms. Use your hands to divide the dough into two balls, one slightly larger than the other, and wrap tightly in plastic. Chill for at least 2 hours or overnight.

2. Preheat the oven to 400°F.

3. Unwrap the pie crusts and set them on a lightly floured surface. The dough may still be crumbly; if it is, use your hands to knead the dough a bit and gather it into a firm disc. Roll out the larger crust to a circle 10 inches in diameter, dusting with flour as necessary to keep it from sticking to your rolling pin. Place it into the bottom of a 9-inch pie plate and trim any excess around the outer edge. Prick the bottom of the crust evenly with fork tines.

4. *For the peach filling:* In a large bowl, combine the peach slices, sugar, almond extract, lemon juice, and tapioca. Fold everything together gently with a rubber spatula. You want the peaches to be evenly coated with the liquids and sugar.

5. Pour the peaches and their juices into the crust.

6. Roll out the second crust to 9 inches in diameter and place it over the pie. Crimp the top crust with the edges of the bottom crust to form a seal, making a decorative pattern with fork tines or your fingers if you'd like. Cut 2 or 3 incisions about 3 inches in length in the top of the pie to allow air to escape when baking. These incisions can be cut in a decorative pattern if desired.

7. In a small bowl, whisk the egg with 1 tablespoon of water. Brush the mixture over the top of the crust so that it has a light coating of egg wash.

8. Set the pie on a rimmed baking sheet and bake it for 50 to 55 minutes or until the crust is golden brown and the pie is hot and bubbly. Allow the pie to cool on a wire rack until it is comfortable to touch. Serve warm.

make-ahead tips: There are 3 ways to make the pie ahead. It can be assembled up to 8 hours before baking. Prepare it in its entirety and cover the top tightly with plastic wrap. It can be left in the refrigerator like this until ready to bake. Alternatively, make the crust ahead of time and prepare the peaches just before baking. The crust will stay refrigerated for up to 3 days, or frozen for up to 6 months. To freeze the unbaked pie, like I do with my mom every summer, wrap the prepared pie in two layers of plastic wrap and an outer layer of aluminum foil. It will keep frozen for up to 6 months. Bring it to room temperature prior to baking.

dutch almond torte

This is my friend Vanessa's childhood comfort food. She remembers her German mother making this classic Dutch dessert for her whenever she was in need of a reminder of home. I learned how to make it at one of Vanessa's cooking classes in Cooperstown. She prepared it in 20 minutes flat, and it was absolutely delicious. I love how the shortbread crust is infused with a sweet almond flavor.

 naptime
stopwatch

20 minutes prep time
40 minutes bake time

makes one 9-inch torte

1 cup (2 sticks) unsalted butter, at room temperature, plus more as needed for the pan

1 cup granulated sugar

2 large eggs, divided

2 cups all-purpose flour, plus more as needed for dusting

1 teaspoon kosher salt

8 ounces pure almond paste

1/3 cup sliced almonds

Confectioners' sugar for dusting

1. Preheat the oven to 325°F. Butter a 9-inch round tart pan with a removable bottom; set aside.

2. In an electric mixer fitted with a paddle attachment, cream the butter and sugar on medium speed until fluffy, about 2 minutes. Add 1 egg and mix until it is incorporated and the mixture looks slightly curdled. With the mixer on low speed, slowly add the flour and salt and mix until just combined. Divide the dough into 2 equal-sized balls. Wrap each in plastic wrap and chill in the refrigerator for 1 hour or up to 1 day.

3. After the dough has chilled, remove it from the refrigerator and allow it to rest for 10 minutes as it comes to room temperature. Using a lightly floured rolling pin, roll out each ball to a circle 9 inches in diameter. Press one of the circles into the tart pan so it covers the bottom evenly and comes 1/4 inch up the sides.

4. Roll out the almond paste into a flat disc about 8 inches in diameter and place it on top of the dough in the tart pan. Take the second circle of dough and place it on top of the almond paste. Pat it down so it covers all of the almond paste and press around the edges to form a seal with the dough on the bottom.

5. In a small bowl, whisk the remaining egg with 1 tablespoon water. Using a pastry brush, sweep the egg wash over the top of the tart, making sure it is evenly covered. Scatter the sliced almonds on top.

6. Bake the torte for 35 to 40 minutes or until the top is lightly golden and the edges are crispy and have pulled away from the sides of the pan. The almonds should be lightly browned and toasted.

7. Allow the torte to cool to room temperature in the pan. To serve, remove it from the pan and dust it lightly with confectioners' sugar.

serving ideas: This torte is the perfect tea time treat or a light dessert. It travels well and is great for taking to friends or potlucks.

make-ahead tips: Making the dough ahead of time and chilling it for up to 1 day will make it easier to assemble the torte when you are ready to bake it. The dough will freeze well, too. Simply wrap it in a double layer of plastic wrap and an outer layer of aluminum foil. It will last this way frozen for up to 3 months.

black bottom peanut butter pie

This pie is like a Reese's Peanut Butter Cup for adults. A rich peanut butter-graham cracker crust cradles thick peanut butter custard with a secret chocolate bottom. The hardest part about making this during naptime is not dipping your finger in for a taste before dinner! Be sure to leave enough time for the pie to chill before eating.

naptime stopwatch

30 minutes prep time

makes one 9-inch pie

2 cups graham cracker crumbs (about 16 crackers pulsed in the food processor)

1 ¼ cups granulated sugar, divided

4 ounces (1 stick) unsalted butter, divided

1 ½ cups smooth peanut butter (not natural-style), divided

3 large egg yolks

2 ¼ cups whole milk

½ cup all-purpose flour

½ teaspoon kosher salt

2 teaspoons vanilla extract

5 ounces semisweet chocolate, divided

1. Preheat the oven to 350°F.

2. In a small bowl, combine the graham cracker crumbs and ½ cup of sugar. Stir to combine and set aside. In a small mixing bowl, melt 6 tablespoons of butter in the microwave and immediately add ¼ cup of the peanut butter while the butter is still hot and stir the mixture until it is completely smooth. Pour this mixture into the bowl with the graham cracker crumbs and mix until the crumbs are evenly moistened. Use your fingertips to press the crumb mixture into the bottom of a 9-inch springform pan or 9-inch deep-dish pie plate, allowing it to go 1 inch up the sides. Bake the crust for 10 minutes, or until it is lightly toasted. Then remove it from the oven and allow it to cool.

3. In a large saucepan over medium heat, combine the egg yolks, milk, remaining ¾ cup sugar, flour, and salt, and whisk continuously until the mixture thickens and has a custard-like consistency, about 8 to 10 minutes. Once the liquid has thickened, remove it from the heat and stir in the remaining 1¼ cups of peanut butter and the vanilla extract until the mixture is completely smooth and silky. Set aside.

4. Melt 4 ounces of the chocolate with the remaining 2 tablespoons butter in a small saucepan over low heat. Once the chocolate is just melted, remove the pan from the heat and stir the chocolate until it is smooth and glossy. Pour the melted chocolate over the prepared crust. Use a knife or spatula to make sure it coats the bottom of the pie evenly. Carefully pour the custard on top of the chocolate layer and use a knife or spatula to smooth the surface of the custard while it is warm.

5. Allow the custard to cool to room temperature for about 1 hour. Then cover it with plastic wrap and chill it in the refrigerator for at least 6 hours before serving. Before serving, shave or finely chop the remaining semisweet chocolate and sprinkle over the pie. Remove the springform side (if using a springform pan) and cut the pie into slices with a sharp knife.

mint chip meringues

These soft, poufy cookies are an ideal sweet treat when you are looking to skimp on calories but not on taste. You will love the crackly exterior and soft, airy inside. They are great for young children since they are so easy to chew. It is a cinch to make them during naptime: Simply whip up the batter, place them in the oven, and forget about them for the next 2 hours.

 naptime stopwatch

15 minutes prep time
1 hour 45 minutes bake time

makes approximately 2 dozen meringues

2 large egg whites

1 teaspoon peppermint extract

¼ teaspoon cream of tartar

1 pinch kosher salt

7 tablespoons superfine sugar, divided

1 cup mini semisweet chocolate chips

1. Preheat the oven to 200°F. Line a baking sheet with parchment paper or a silicone liner.

2. In an electric mixer fitted with a whisk attachment, beat the egg whites, peppermint extract, cream of tartar, and salt on medium speed until they are light and foamy, about 4 minutes. With the mixer on high speed, carefully add 4 tablespoons of the sugar and continue beating on high until the whites hold stiff peaks, about 8 to 10 minutes.

3. Turn off the mixer and very gently sprinkle the remaining 3 tablespoons of sugar on top of the egg whites and fold them it in with the chocolate chips. When everything is just combined, stop folding so you don't deflate the egg whites.

4. Dollop the mixture in heaping tablespoonfuls about 2 inches apart on the baking sheets. Bake the meringues for 1 hour and 45 minutes, or until they are firm to the touch, but not brown.

serving ideas: These are a fun treat for Christmas time. Sprinkle the tops with crushed candy canes before they bake to make them extra festive.

variation ideas: For regular chocolate chip meringues, substitute vanilla extract for peppermint extract.

sour cream & almond cookies

Last summer when I visited my friend Veronica in Cooperstown she served these cookies. They were soft and creamy with just a hint of cinnamon. Veronica was able to write down the recipe off the top of her head because she has made them so many times. She grew up making them with her mother, Julia Gil, and often hands out the recipe to eager recipients. After you eat one you'll understand why.

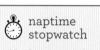

naptime stopwatch

12 minutes prep time
30 minutes bake time

makes approximately
5 dozen cookies

3 cups all-purpose flour

1 teaspoon baking powder

½ teaspoon baking soda

½ teaspoon kosher salt

1 teaspoon ground cinnamon, divided

1 cup (2 sticks) unsalted butter, at room temperature

1½ cups plus 1 teaspoon granulated sugar, divided

2 large eggs

1 cup full-fat sour cream, stirred well

1 teaspoon almond extract

1. Sift together the flour, baking powder, baking soda, salt, and ½ teaspoon of cinnamon into a large bowl and set aside.

2. In an electric mixer fitted with the paddle attachment, cream the butter and 1½ cups of sugar on medium speed until light and fluffy, about 2 minutes. Add the eggs and beat again until frothy. Add the sour cream and almond extract and beat the mixture until it is smooth and creamy and everything is combined. Scrape down the sides of the mixing bowl as needed.

3. With the mixer on low speed, slowly add the flour mixture until it is completely combined.

4. Transfer the batter to a sheet of plastic wrap. Wrap it tightly so that no air can reach it, and chill it in the refrigerator for at least 2 hours, or up to 1 day.

5. Preheat the oven to 375°F. Line a cookie sheet with parchment paper or a silicone liner. Drop the batter in rounded tablespoonfuls onto the cookie sheet at least 2 inches apart.

6. In a small bowl, whisk together the remaining teaspoon of sugar and ½ teaspoon of cinnamon. Lightly and evenly sprinkle the top of each cookie with the cinnamon-sugar mixture. Bake the cookies for 10 to 12 minutes, or until the edges of the cookies are lightly browned and the tops begin to freckle.

make-ahead tips: This dough can chill for up to a day in the refrigerator. Avoid freezing it, though, which will change the texture of the sour cream.

serving ideas: The sophistication of these cookies makes them appropriate for serving at an afternoon tea or luncheon. They are also great for young children; their light texture is very easy to chew.

variation ideas: If almond flavoring is not your thing, you can substitute vanilla extract or, for more fun, hazelnut extract.

orange sugar cookies

I've always loved the combination of citrus and sugar, which is why I added orange zest to these classic cookies. They are perfect for having around the house for snacking or serving to friends. In order for the orange flavor to really blossom, the dough should be chilled for at least 6 hours before baking.

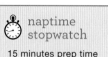 **naptime stopwatch**

15 minutes prep time
12 minutes bake time

makes approximately
2 dozen cookies

4 ounces (1 stick) unsalted butter, at room temperature

1 cup granulated sugar, divided

⅓ cup packed light brown sugar

2 large eggs

2 tablespoons freshly grated orange zest (from about 2 medium oranges), divided

2 cups all-purpose flour, plus more as needed for dusting

1½ teaspoons baking powder

1 pinch kosher salt

1. In an electric mixer fitted with a paddle attachment, cream the butter, ½ cup granulated sugar, and the brown sugar until light and fluffy, about 2 minutes. Add the eggs one at a time and mix until combined, then add 1 tablespoon of orange zest and mix until incorporated.

2. In a separate bowl, combine the flour, baking powder, and salt. With the mixer on low, slowly add the flour mixture to the batter bit by bit until it is just incorporated and dough comes together. Wrap the dough in plastic and chill for at least 6 hours.

3. Meanwhile, make the orange sugar: Combine the remaining table-spoon of orange zest and the remaining ½ cup sugar in a mini-chopper or food processor and pulse until the zest and sugar are finely ground and completely incorporated. You will notice when this happens because there is a burst of orange fragrance in your kitchen as the oils are released!

4. Once the dough has chilled, preheat the oven to 375°F. Line baking sheets with parchment paper or a silicone liner.

5. Generously flour a work surface and a rolling pin and roll the dough to ¼-inch thickness. Use a 2-inch round cookie cutter to cut out the cookies, rerolling the dough as necessary until it has all been used. Place the cut cookies onto the prepared baking sheets. Sprinkle each cookie with an even dusting of orange sugar.

6. Bake the cookies for 9 to 11 minutes, or until the centers of the cookies are set and the tops are very light golden brown. Transfer cookies to a wire rack to cool and serve.

make-ahead tips: This dough can be frozen for up to 3 months when wrapped in a double layer of plastic wrap and an outer layer of aluminum foil.

birthday cookies

When anyone in our family celebrates a birthday, my mother makes these cookies. She cuts the rich, buttery dough with a cookie cutter shaped in the number of the recipient's age, and dots the cookie with the same number of chocolate candies. There is nothing sweeter then receiving a nice big plate of these—they are the best way to herald in a new year. This delicate batter requires 1 hour of chilling time before baking.

 naptime stopwatch

15 minutes prep time
10 minutes bake time

makes about 20 cookies

cookies

2 ½ cups all-purpose flour, plus more as needed for dusting

1 teaspoon baking soda

1 teaspoon baking powder

1 teaspoon cream of tartar

¼ teaspoon kosher salt

1 cup (2 sticks) unsalted butter, at room temperature

1 ½ cups confectioners' sugar

1 large egg

1 teaspoon vanilla extract

frosting

¼ cup (½ stick) unsalted butter, at room temperature

1 ½ cups confectioners' sugar

½ teaspoon vanilla extract

3 to 5 teaspoons whole milk, or as needed

Food coloring (optional)

Chocolate candies, such as M&M's or chocolate chips

1. *To make the cookies:* In a large bowl, combine the flour, baking soda, baking powder, cream of tartar, and salt. Stir with a whisk to combine and set aside.

2. In an electric mixer fitted with a paddle attachment, cream the butter and sugar on medium speed until light and fluffy, about 2 minutes. Reduce the mixer to low, slowly add the egg and vanilla extract and mix until everything is combined.

3. Continuing with the mixer on low, add in the dry ingredients until they are just combined and the flour is no longer visible. Transfer the dough to a large piece of plastic wrap. Form a ball and wrap it tightly in the plastic. Chill the dough in the refrigerator for at least 1 hour or up to a day.

4. Preheat the oven to 375°F. Line a baking sheet with parchment paper or a silicone liner and set aside.

5. Generously flour a clean surface and a rolling pin. Roll out the chilled dough to ⅛-inch thickness. Use cookie cutters to cut out the shapes. Gather any scraps of dough into a second ball and roll it out again to ⅛-inch thickness until all the dough has been used.

6. Place the cut cookies on the prepared baking sheet and bake for 10 to 12 minutes, or until the cookies have puffed up slightly and are golden brown around the edges. Cool cookies for a minute on the sheet then transfer to a wire rack to cool completely.

7. *To make the frosting:* Using an electric mixer, cream the butter, sugar and vanilla extract on medium speed until smooth, about 2 minutes. Add the milk one teaspoon at a time until the frosting is a spreadable consistency. It should still hold a peak when swiped with a spatula. If you'd like to color the frosting, add a few drops of food coloring and mix until you reach the desired color.

8. Spread a thin layer of frosting on each cookie and dot with chocolate candies. Happy Birthday!

serving ideas: The birthday numbers are perfect for situations where you can't have a cake. I take these into Daphne's preschool classroom for her birthday snack: a nice change from cupcakes.

variation ideas: Though we use this recipe primarily for birthday celebrations, they can be used at any time of the year with any kind of cookie cutter. We often have cookie decorating afternoons with Daphne and her friends. I roll out the dough and the kids cut the cookies into desired shapes and decorate them with frosting and all kinds of sanding sugars.

double-chocolate espresso cookies

After Daphne was born I revised my method for making cookies. I made the dough during naptime, let it rest in the fridge, and baked them after she went to bed. Not only was breaking up the baking process more manageable, but it also taught me a very important lesson: Cookies taste better when the dough has been allowed to rest before baking. Once I realized this I started making all of my cookie dough in advance. The cookies taste much better for it.

naptime stopwatch

15 minutes prep time
10 minutes bake time

makes approximately
4 dozen cookies

2½ cups all-purpose flour

¾ cup unsweetened cocoa powder

2 tablespoons instant espresso powder

1 teaspoon kosher salt

1 teaspoon baking soda

10 ounces (2¼ sticks), unsalted butter, at room temperature

1 cup granulated sugar

1 cup tightly packed light brown sugar

2 large eggs, at room temperature

1 (12 ounce-package) semi-sweet chocolate chunks

1. In a mixing bowl, whisk together the flour, cocoa powder, espresso powder, salt, and baking soda and set aside.

2. In an electric mixer fitted with the paddle attachment, cream the butter and both sugars on medium speed until light and fluffy, about 2 minutes. Add the eggs one at a time, beating well after each addition. Turn off the mixer and scrape down the sides and bottom of the bowl with a rubber spatula.

3. With the mixer on low speed, slowly add the dry ingredients to the wet ingredients until the dough is combined, stopping the mixer to scrape down the sides as needed. Once the last of the dry ingredients is mixed in, turn off the machine. (Do not overbeat the batter.) Using a wooden spoon, mix in the chocolate chips. Transfer the dough to plastic wrap and wrap the dough tightly so that no air is able to reach it. Place it in the refrigerator and chill for at least 4 hours or up to 3 days.

4. Preheat the oven to 350°F. Line a baking sheet with parchment paper or a silicone liner and set aside. Bring the dough to room temperature for about 15 minutes and drop it by the rounded teaspoonful onto the lined cookie sheet, 2 inches apart. Bake the cookies for 10 to 12 minutes, or until the centers are set. Cool on a wire rack and serve.

make-ahead tips: The dough will hold for up to 2 days before it needs to be baked. It can also be frozen for up to 6 weeks before baking. To freeze it, wrap it in 2 layers of plastic wrap and cover it with a layer of aluminum foil.

serving tips: These cookies are great to serve to friends and family, especially if they are sleep deprived! Try sandwiching vanilla ice cream between them to make Double-Chocolate Espresso Ice Cream Sandwiches, perfect for casual outdoor barbecues.

variation ideas: It is perfectly fine if you want to eliminate the espresso powder and just make these Double-Chocolate Cookies for the kids. They will love them just as much and never know what they're missing.

gingersnaps

This is an over-the-top version of my favorite holiday cookie. I made my favorite gingersnap recipe spicier and chewier and added crystallized ginger. A friend of mine took them to work once, and his co-workers e-mailed him requesting the recipe! They are bound to be a huge hit at your house, too. Remember that the dough needs to chill for at least 4 hours, so plan ahead.

naptime stopwatch

15 minutes prep time
10 minutes bake time

makes approximately
4 dozen cookies

6 ounces (1 ½ sticks) unsalted butter, at room temperature

1 ¼ cups granulated sugar, divided

1 large egg

¼ cup dark molasses

2 ¼ cups all-purpose flour

2 teaspoons baking soda

½ teaspoon ground cloves

1 teaspoon ground ginger

1 teaspoon ground cinnamon

¼ teaspoon kosher salt

¾ cup finely chopped crystallized ginger

1. In an electric mixer fitted with a paddle attachment, cream the butter and 1 cup of sugar on medium-low speed until light and fluffy, about 2 minutes. Add the egg and molasses and mix on medium speed until just combined. The batter will look slightly curdled at this point.

2. In a separate bowl, whisk together the flour, baking soda, cloves, ginger, cinnamon, and salt.

3. Scrape down the sides of the mixing bowl with a rubber spatula. With the mixer on low speed, add the dry ingredients a few tablespoons at a time until everything is completely combined. Do not overbeat or the cookies will be tough when they are baked. Using a wooden spoon, stir the crystallized ginger into the batter.

4. Transfer the dough to plastic wrap and wrap the dough tightly so that no air is able to reach it. Place it in the refrigerator and chill for at least 4 hours or up to 3 days.

5. Preheat the oven to 350°F. Line a baking sheet with parchment paper or a silicone liner and set aside. Remove the batter from the refrigerator and allow it to soften at room temperature for about 15 minutes.

6. Pour the remaining ¼ cup sugar into a shallow bowl. Pinch off balls of dough, about 1 teaspoon each, and roll them between the palms of your hands. Drop each ball in the bowl of sugar and roll it around until it is completely coated. Shake off any excess sugar and place the balls 2 inches apart on the prepared baking sheet. Bake for 10 to 12 minutes, or until the edges are darkened and the center of the cookie is set. Transfer cookies to a wire rack to cool completely.

make-ahead tips: This dough freezes well if you are making it ahead of time for the holiday season. To freeze, pat the dough into a ball, and wrap in two layers of plastic wrap followed by a layer of aluminum foil. It will keep in the freezer for up to 3 months.

variation ideas: The sturdy, cakey textures of these cookies make them great candidates for cookie sandwiches. In the summer, place a scoop of your favorite ice cream in the middle to make Gingersnap Ice Cream Sandwiches. In the winter, a simple lemon buttercream frosting transforms them into creamy Ginger-Lemon Sandwiches.

brown sugar apple cookies with cider glaze

My childhood neighbor, Katie Sanford, is like a second mother to me. I've known her my entire life and her family kitchen is as familiar to me as my own. As a busy mother of two, she often did her baking while her kids were sleeping late on weekends. I always wondered why she had cookies cooling on the counter when I wandered over after breakfast. She recently explained to me she would make the dough the day before and let it chill all night, then bake the cookies fresh before everyone woke up!

naptime
stopwatch

15 minutes prep time
12 minutes bake time

makes approximately
4 dozen cookies

cookies

2 ¼ cups all-purpose flour

1 teaspoon baking soda

1 teaspoon ground cinnamon

½ teaspoon ground cloves

½ teaspoon ground nutmeg

½ teaspoon kosher salt

4 ounces (1 stick) unsalted
butter, at room temperature

1 ⅓ cups tightly packed dark
brown sugar

1 large egg

¼ cup whole milk

1 medium Granny Smith
apple, peeled, cored, and
grated (about 1 cup)

(continued)

1. *To make the cookies:* In a mixing bowl, combine the flour, baking soda, cinnamon, cloves, nutmeg, and salt and stir them together with a whisk.

2. In an electric mixer fitted with the paddle attachment, cream the butter and sugar until smooth on medium speed, about 2 minutes. Using a rubber spatula, scrape down the sides of the bowl then mix in the egg and the milk. The batter will look slightly curdled at this point.

3. With the mixer on low, slowly add the dry ingredients, mixing until everything is just combined and no more flour is visible, scraping down the sides of the bowl as needed. Turn off the mixer and stir the grated apple into the batter with a wooden spoon. Wrap the dough tightly in plastic wrap and refrigerate it for at least 4 hours or up to one day.

4. Preheat the oven to 350°F. Line 2 baking sheets with parchment paper or a silicone liner and set aside.

5. Drop cookies by the rounded teaspoonful 2 inches apart onto the lined baking sheets. Dip your fingertips in water and press the cookies down slightly so that the tops are flat. Bake them for 12 to 14 minutes, or until the cookies hold their shape and are slightly darkened around the edges. Transfer the cookies to a wire rack with a kitchen towel underneath it and allow the cookies to cool completely before adding the glaze.

6. *To make the glaze:* In a mixing bowl, stir together the confectioners' sugar, cider, and cinnamon until completely smooth. The glaze should be a little thin, not thick like a frosting. If you want a thicker glaze, add an additional ½ cup of confectioners' sugar.

7. To glaze the cookies, spoon the glaze over the cooled cookies while they are still on a wire rack. Let them sit for 10 minutes, or until the glaze is just set.

make-ahead tips: This batter keeps well when made ahead of time. Wrap it in plastic and store it in the refrigerator for up to 3 days, or frozen (wrapped in 2 layers of plastic and an outer layer of aluminum foil) for up to 3 months.

serving ideas: This is an ideal cookie for fall. I love serving it at fall gatherings or even as a nibble after Thanksgiving dinner. Sandwich a scoop of vanilla ice cream between two cookies for particularly fun dessert. It tastes just like apple pie with ice cream, only in cookie form!

variation ideas: If you want a crunchier cookie, add 1 cup of finely chopped walnuts when you stir in the shredded apples.

glaze

3 cups confectioners' sugar

$\frac{1}{3}$ cup apple cider

$\frac{1}{4}$ teaspoon ground cinnamon

lemon coconut squares with shortbread crust

These are great for summer picnics. Everyone loves how the tart lemon and sweet coconut create a tropical flavor. They stand up well to bumpy rides in the tote bag, making them perfect for taking on the go. For the complete picnic meal I serve them alongside a generous scoop of Ruth's Curry Chicken Salad (page 54), soft rolls, and crisp white wine.

naptime
stopwatch

15 minutes prep time
35 minutes bake time

makes 2 dozen squares

bars

4 ounces (1 stick) unsalted butter, at room temperature, plus more as needed for the pan

1 ½ cups plus 2 tablespoons all-purpose flour, sifted and divided, plus more as needed for the pan

1 ½ cups packed light brown sugar, divided

2 large eggs, lightly beaten

1 ½ cups sweetened shredded coconut

½ teaspoon baking soda

½ teaspoon vanilla extract

¼ teaspoon kosher salt

glaze

1 tablespoon unsalted butter, melted and cooled

1 cup confectioners' sugar

Juice of 1 medium lemon

1. Preheat the oven to 275°F. Butter and flour a 13 x 9-inch baking dish and set aside.

2. *To make the bars:* In a mixing bowl, combine the butter, 1½ cups flour, and ½ cup brown sugar and work together with your hands until a crumble begins to form. Press the dough into the bottom of the prepared baking pan and bake for 12 to 15 minutes, or until the edges are lightly browned.

3. While the crust is baking, make the filling: In a separate bowl, combine the eggs, remaining 1 cup brown sugar, coconut, the remaining 2 tablespoons of flour, baking soda, vanilla, and salt. Using a wooden spoon, stir the ingredients until everything is combined.

4. When the crust has finished baking, remove it from the oven and allow it to cool for 10 minutes. Increase the oven temperature to 350°F.

5. Spread the coconut filling evenly over the cooled crust. Bake for 22 to 25 minutes, or until the coconut is golden brown and the top is set.

6. *While the coconut filling is baking, make the glaze:* In a small mixing bowl, whisk together the melted butter, confectioners' sugar, and lemon juice until completely smooth.

7. When the bars have finished baking, remove them from the oven and drizzle the top evenly with the glaze while the bars are still warm. The glaze will sink into the squares and seem to disappear from sight. This is exactly what you want!

8. Allow the bars to cool in the pan uncovered for 1 hour, then cover the pan with plastic wrap and refrigerate it for 2 hours, until they are set. Cut into 2-inch squares and serve.

make-ahead tips: These are ideal to make at least a few hours before you want to serve them since they need time to cool and set. Once ready they travel very well and will stay fresh for several days in a sealed container in the refrigerator.

blueberry hazelnut oatmeal squares

When I first wrote about the rhubarb version of these squares on my blog I got a resounding response. Turns out there are plenty of rhubarb fans out there just like me! When Daphne was born, I started making these with fresh blueberries since she prefers those to rhubarb. I always have to hide them after I bake them during naptime. If she knows they are in the kitchen she'll ask if she can skip dinner and go straight to dessert. Plan on letting the oatmeal squares chill at least 2 hours before serving.

 naptime stopwatch

20 minutes prep time
30 minutes bake time

makes 2 dozen squares

⅔ cup granulated sugar

¼ cup orange juice

2 tablespoons cornstarch

3½ cups fresh blueberries (or 1 pound frozen blueberries, thawed)

1 teaspoon vanilla extract

1½ cups quick-cooking oats

1½ cups all-purpose flour

⅔ cup packed dark brown sugar

½ cup finely chopped toasted hazelnuts

½ teaspoon baking soda

¼ teaspoon ground nutmeg

6 ounces (1½ sticks) unsalted butter, at room temperature, cut into small cubes, plus more as needed

1. Preheat the oven to 350°F. Butter a 13 x 9-inch baking dish and set aside.

2. In a small saucepan over medium heat, combine the sugar, orange juice, and cornstarch and cook until the sugar is dissolved. Add the blueberries and vanilla and cook until the berry mixture begins to thicken, stirring constantly, about 8 to 10 minutes. You will know the mixture is finished when it develops a thick, jam-like consistency. Remove from the heat and allow the pan to cool.

3. In a large bowl, combine the oats, flour, sugar, hazelnuts, baking soda, and nutmeg. Then add the butter pieces and use your fingers to work the butter into the dry ingredients until the mixture is all pea-sized lumps.

4. Firmly pat three-quarters of the oatmeal mixture into the bottom of the prepared pan, reserving one-quarter of the mixture to use as topping. Pour the blueberry mixture over the oatmeal crust and spread it evenly over the crust with a spatula. Sprinkle the top of the blueberry mixture evenly with the remaining oatmeal mixture.

5. Bake the bars for 30 to 35 minutes, or until the oatmeal topping begins to brown.

6. Remove from the oven and allow the pan to cool to room temperature. Then cover it and refrigerate the bars until chilled, about 2 hours. Use a sharp knife to slice them into 2-inch squares and serve.

serving ideas: For dessert, serve the bars with some ice cream or whipped cream. For breakfast, eat them with a scoop of Greek yogurt.

variation ideas: Rhubarb can be substituted for the blueberries. Chop the stalks into 1-inch pieces before stewing them on the stovetop.

grammie's seven layer bars

Grammie Garwood passed this recipe down to each of her grandchildren. I am lucky that one of her grandchildren shared the recipe with me. These dense, fudgy bars are the perfect sweet treat to keep around the house or package up to give to friends. Since chilling time is required before eating, it is best to bake these at least 2 hours before you intend to serve them.

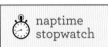

naptime stopwatch

10 minutes prep time
35 minutes bake time

makes 2 dozen bars

4 ounces (1 stick) unsalted butter, melted and cooled

1 cup graham cracker crumbs (from about 8 crackers pulsed in the food processor)

1 cup shredded sweetened coconut

1 (12-ounce) package semisweet chocolate chips

1 (12-ounce) package butterscotch chips

1 (14-ounce) can sweetened condensed milk

1 cup coarsely chopped pecans

1. Preheat the oven to 350°F.

2. Pour the melted butter into the bottom of a 13 x 9-inch baking dish and swirl the pan so that the bottom is evenly coated with butter, paying special attention to the corners.

3. Sprinkle the graham cracker crumbs evenly over the butter and press down with your fingertips to form a very thin crust. Create even layers on top of the graham crackers with the remaining ingredients in this order: shredded coconut, chocolate chips, butterscotch chips, sweetened condensed milk, and chopped pecans on top.

4. Bake the bars for 35 to 40 minutes, or until the ingredients have completely melted together to form one uniform batter.

5. Remove the pan from the oven and allow it to cool to room temperature. Then cover it with plastic wrap and place it in the refrigerator for 2 hours, or until the bars have chilled and are completely solid.

6. Cut the bars into 2-inch squares with a sharp knife and store them in a container lined with waxed paper.

serving ideas: The childlike appeal of these bars makes them perfect for family gatherings, school treats, or picnics.

Opposite page, clockwise from top: Uncle Will's Dirty Blondies, page 175; Grammie's Seven Layer Bars, this page; German Chocolate Brownies, page 174

german chocolate brownies

I think brownies are one of the best desserts around. I always love to find new ways to make them even more decadent and indulgent. One day I decided to top my favorite brownies with some German frosting. It was an experiment that yielded delicious results; taste them for yourself.

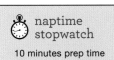

naptime stopwatch

10 minutes prep time
40 minutes bake time

makes 2 dozen squares

brownies

6 ounces dark chocolate (at least 72% cacao), coarsely chopped

6 ounces (1 ½ sticks) unsalted butter, plus more as needed for the pan

2½ cups granulated sugar

2 teaspoons vanilla extract

4 large eggs, at room temperature

1 ½ cups all-purpose flour

½ teaspoon sea salt

frosting

4 ounces (1 stick) unsalted butter

½ cup packed dark brown sugar

¼ cup heavy cream

3 cups (12 ounces) coarsely chopped walnuts

3 cups shredded sweetened coconut

1. Preheat the oven to 375°F. Butter a 13 x 9-inch baking dish and set aside.

2. *To make the brownies:* Place a large heatproof bowl over a saucepan of simmering water, making sure the water does not touch the bottom of the bowl. Add the chopped chocolate and the butter to the bowl and stir them with a heatproof spatula or wooden spoon until they are completely melted into a smooth ganache. Remove the bowl from the heat about 5 minutes later.

3. Allow the chocolate mixture to cool for 2 minutes, then stir the sugar and vanilla; it is OK if the mixture seems a little gritty. Add the eggs one at a time, stirring well after each addition. Finally, add the flour and the salt and stir the mixture until all of the ingredients are completely incorporated and the flour is no longer visible.

4. Pour the batter into the prepared baking dish and bake it for 25 to 27 minutes, or until a cake tester comes out clean. Allow the brownies to cool for 10 minutes.

5. *While the brownies are baking, make the frosting:* Melt the butter in the microwave or on the stove and stir in the brown sugar and cream until everything is completely incorporated. Add the walnuts and coconut and mix well. Set aside until the brownies are ready. The frosting will look thick but will soften when heated under the broiler.

6. After the brownies have cooled for 10 minutes, turn the broiler on to the high-heat setting. Spread the walnut frosting evenly over the top. Place the pan under the broiler for about 2 minutes, watching carefully the entire time. The walnuts will begin to darken and the mixture will bubble. Remove the brownies before the walnuts burn. Allow the brownies to cool completely before cutting into 2-inch squares.

variation ideas: Pecans can be substituted if walnuts are unavailable. To make the frosting chocolaty, add in ½ cup of semisweet chocolate chips.

uncle will's dirty blondies

My brother Will got this recipe at summer camp when he was twelve. He was so smitten with the brown sugar blondies the cafeteria served, he wrote down the cook's recipe on a scrap of paper and brought it home to my mother! Needless to say, she got a huge kick out of his request for Dirty Blondies and has been making these for us ever since. I can't get enough of their wonderful gooey texture. They are one of those childlike treats that adults love.

 naptime stopwatch

10 minutes prep time
20 minutes bake time

makes 16 squares

¼ cup (½ stick) unsalted butter, melted and cooled, plus more as needed for the pan

1 cup packed dark brown sugar

1 large egg

1 teaspoon vanilla extract

1 cup all-purpose flour

1 teaspoon baking soda

1 cup semisweet chocolate chips

1. Preheat the oven to 375°F. Butter a 9 x 9-inch baking pan and set aside.

2. In an electric mixer fitted with the paddle attachment, cream the melted butter and brown sugar until light and fluffy, about 2 minutes. Add the egg and vanilla extract and continue to mix on medium speed until everything is well combined. Reduce the mixer speed to low and add the flour and baking soda, mixing until the flour is just incorporated and the batter is smooth and creamy. Turn off the mixer and stir in the chocolate chips.

3. Pour the batter into the prepared baking dish and bake for 20 minutes, or until the tops of the blondies are browned and set. Allow the blondies to cool completely before cutting them into 2-inch squares and serving.

serving ideas: This traditional camp dessert makes a fabulous base for an ice cream sundae. Top it with ice cream and dulce de leche for a fantastic dessert!

variation ideas: 1 cup of chopped walnuts can be added to the batter for an extra nutty crunch.

pumpkin spice bars
with maple cream cheese frosting

The rich pumpkin spice and maple frosting are the epitome of fall. I stock up on cans of pumpkin purée each autumn and make these for Thanksgiving and Christmas.

naptime stopwatch

15 minutes prep time
30 minutes bake time

makes 2 dozen squares

bars

Butter as needed for the pan

2 cups all-purpose flour

2 teaspoons baking powder

1 teaspoons baking soda

1 teaspoon pumpkin pie spice

1 teaspoon kosher salt

4 large eggs, at room temperature

1 ⅔ cups sugar

1 cup vegetable oil

1 (14 ounce-can) pure organic pumpkin purée, or the equivalent amount of fresh pumpkin purée, drained in a fine-mesh sieve if particularly wet

(continued)

1. Preheat the oven to 350°F. Butter a 13 x 9-inch baking dish and set aside.

2. *To make the bars:* In a mixing bowl, whisk together the flour, baking powder, baking soda, pumpkin pie spice, and salt and set aside.

3. In an electric mixer fitted with the paddle attachment, mix the eggs, sugar, oil, and pumpkin purée on medium speed until completely smooth and blended, about 2 minutes.

4. With the mixer on low speed, add the dry ingredients to the wet ingredients until they are fully combined. Stop the mixer once or twice to scrape down the sides of the bowl with a rubber spatula.

5. Spread the batter in the prepared pan and bake for 25 to 30 minutes, or until the center is set and a cake tester comes out clean. Allow the bars to cool to room temperature in the pan before frosting.

6. *To make the frosting:* In an electric mixer fitted with the paddle attachment, on medium-high speed cream the cream cheese, butter, vanilla, and maple syrup until completely smooth, about 2 minutes. The frosting will look curdled initially, but will gradually become creamy and uniform. Add the confectioners' sugar and blend well until frosting is thickened and there are no visible lumps, about 1 more minute.

7. To frost the bars, dip a small offset spatula in warm water and dry it well. Gently spread some of the frosting over the cake in the pan, smoothing it quickly. Continue frosting, dipping the spatula in warm water as needed. Cut into squares and serve.

make-ahead tips: These bars are moist enough to be made up to a day before you want to serve them. Once the pan has cooled, cover it tightly with plastic wrap to maintain freshness. Frost them and cut into 2-inch squares just before serving.

serving ideas: For Halloween, dot the frosting with candy corn or black and orange sprinkles. At Thanksgiving or Christmas, give them a light dusting of cinnamon for a more sophisticated look.

frosting

4 ounces cream cheese, at room temperature

4 ounces (1 stick) unsalted butter, at room temperature

1 teaspoon vanilla extract

2 tablespoons pure maple syrup

2 cups confectioners' sugar, sifted

everyday cream puffs

Cream puffs are one of those desserts everyone will think you slaved over but are really incredibly easy to make. I like to bake the puffs during naptime and make the fillings right before we want to eat. The versatility of the fluffy egg puffs offers endless possibilities: fill them with flavored whipped cream for a traditional approach, or give them a French twist by adding ice cream to make profiteroles.

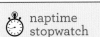

naptime stopwatch

10 minutes prep time
40 minutes bake time

makes 10 puffs

puffs

4 ounces (1 stick) unsalted butter

1 cup all-purpose flour

1 teaspoon granulated sugar

1 teaspoon kosher salt

4 large eggs

whipped cream

1 1/2 cups heavy whipping cream

1/4 cup confectioners' sugar, plus more as needed for dusting

1 teaspoon vanilla extract

1. Preheat the oven to 400°F.

2. *To make the puffs:* In a small saucepan over medium-high heat, bring 1 cup water and the butter to a rolling boil. When it reaches the boiling point, add the flour, sugar, and salt to the pan and stir vigorously with a wooden spoon until the mixture forms a ball of thick dough.

3. When the dough comes together, immediately remove it from the heat and transfer the dough to a large bowl. Using a wooden spoon, stir in the eggs. As you do this, the batter will look messy and curdled at first, but keep beating and a smooth dough will form in about 1 minute.

4. Use a 1 1/2-inch cookie scoop to drop the dough by the scant 1/4-cup onto 2 ungreased cookie sheets 3 inches apart. Bake the puffs for 35 to 40 minutes or until the dough is puffed, golden, and feels hollow when tapped. If you're unsure as to whether or not the puffs are done, cut through the center of one with a knife: the interior should be moist but cooked through. Allow the puffs to cool on a wire rack until they come to room temperature.

5. *To make the whipped cream:* In a mixing bowl, combine the heavy cream, sugar, and vanilla extract. Using an electric mixer on high speed (or by hand with a whisk), beat until soft peaks form, about 3 minutes.

6. To assemble, slice the puffs in half and fill them with dollops of whipped cream. Sandwich the puffs back together, dust with confectioners' sugar, and serve.

make-ahead tips: These puff should be made the day you intend to serve them. They can be prepared up to 6 hours in advance of serving and should be stored in an airtight container at room temperature until then.

serving ideas: These always make an elegant dessert. For a fun Christmas treat serve them with a scoop of chocolate ice cream, drizzle them with Peppermint Hot Fudge Sauce (page 212), and dust them with some crushed candy canes. For a brunch gathering, fill the puffs with whipped cream and drizzle a bit of chocolate sauce on the outside to resemble an éclair.

variation ideas: To make chocolate whipped cream, add 3 tablespoons of cocoa powder to the heavy cream while it is being beaten with the sugar.

gingerbread cupcakes
with meyer lemon glaze

I like a bold-tasting gingerbread during the holidays, which is why I ramped up the spices in these cupcakes. They make great treats for friends and parties. I often bake them when Daphne is asleep and add the glaze right before serving.

naptime stopwatch

10 minutes prep time
20 minutes bake time

makes 1 dozen
cupcakes

cupcakes

1½ cups all-purpose flour

1 teaspoon baking soda

1 teaspoon ground ginger

1 teaspoon ground cinnamon

1 teaspoon ground nutmeg

¼ teaspoon ground cloves

¼ teaspoon kosher salt

5 tablespoons unsalted butter,
at room temperature

½ cup granulated sugar

½ cup molasses

2 large eggs

½ cup cultured buttermilk

(continued)

1. Preheat the oven to 350°F. Butter or line a 12-cup muffin tin with paper liners.

2. *To make the cupcakes:* Combine the flour, baking soda, ginger, cinnamon, nutmeg, cloves, and salt in a large bowl; stir with a whisk to combine.

3. In an electric mixer fitted with a paddle attachment, cream the butter and sugar on medium speed until light and fluffy, about 2 minutes. Add the molasses and both eggs and mix well, then add the buttermilk and mix until everything is combined.

4. Using a rubber spatula, scrape down the sides of the bowl then reduce the mixer speed to low and slowly add the flour mixture until the batter is smooth and everything is just incorporated.

5. Divide the batter among the muffin cups, filling each to about three-quarters full, and bake for 20 minutes, or until the cupcakes are set and the tops spring back when touched. Allow the cupcakes to cool for 2 minutes in the muffin tins and then transfer to a wire rack to cool completely.

6. *To make the glaze:* In a small mixing bowl, whisk together the confectioners' sugar, lemon juice and zest, and about 1 to 2 tablespoons of water until completely smooth. Add 1 tablespoon of water to start, only adding the second tablespoon if necessary. The glaze should be runny enough for drizzling.

7. Once the cupcakes are completely cooled, drizzle the glaze evenly over the top of each cupcake or dip each cupcake top in the glaze and serve.

make-ahead tips: The cupcakes can be made up to a day ahead of being glazed. Store them in a sealed container until they are ready to be iced.

serving ideas: Cupcakes are always fun to serve at parties and these are particularly festive at holiday gatherings. People will go wild for their strong gingerbread flavor and sweet citrus glaze!

variation ideas: Regular lemons can be substituted if Meyer lemons are unavailable.

glaze

1 ½ cups confectioners' sugar

Juice and zest of 1 medium Meyer lemon

raspberry lime bundt cake with lime glaze

This is a favorite summer cake. I love the dense pound cake-like texture and the combination of citrus and berry flavors. I always make it when we have an excess of fresh raspberries on hand in the summer. It is great for taking to friends or for entertaining.

naptime stopwatch

20 minutes prep time
1 hour 30 minutes bake time

makes 1 bundt cake

All-purpose flour, as needed

3 1/2 cups cake flour

1/2 teaspoon baking powder

1/4 teaspoon salt

12 ounces (3 sticks) unsalted butter, at room temperature, plus more as needed

2 1/4 cups granulated sugar, divided

6 large eggs

1 cup whole milk

4 teaspoons freshly grated lime zest, divided

1 teaspoon vanilla extract

3 cups fresh or frozen raspberries, thawed if frozen

1/2 cup freshly squeezed lime juice

1. Preheat the oven to 350°F. Butter and flour a 10-inch Bundt pan and set aside.

2. In a small bowl, whisk together the cake flour, baking powder, and salt and set aside.

3. In an electric mixer fitted with a paddle attachment, beat the butter on medium speed until it is light and fluffy, about 2 minutes. Reduce the speed and pour in 1 3/4 cups sugar and cream it with the butter until light and fluffy, about 2 minutes. Add the eggs one at a time, beating well after each addition. Scrape down the sides of the bowl, if needed.

4. With the mixer on low, add the flour mixture, alternating with the milk in three additions, ending with the flour. Beat in 2 teaspoons of the lime zest and the vanilla extract. Turn off the mixer and use a rubber spatula to carefully stir in the raspberries.

5. Pour the batter into the prepared Bundt pan and use a spatula to smooth the top of the batter. Bake the cake for 1 hour and 30 minutes or until the cake begins to pull away from the sides of the pan and a wooden pick inserted in the center comes out clean. Let the cake cool in the pan on a wire rack for 20 minutes, then turn it out onto the rack and set it right-side up out of the pan on a plate or cake stand.

6. In a saucepan, combine the remaining 1/2 cup sugar, remaining 2 teaspoons lime zest, and lime juice and bring to a boil over medium heat until the sugar is dissolved. Remove from the heat and let stand for 5 minutes. Brush the lime mixture over the warm cake and let cool completely before serving.

make-ahead tips: This cake freezes well. Wrap it in 2 layers of plastic wrap and a layer of aluminum foil before storing it on an even surface in the freezer. It will last frozen for up to 3 months. Bring to room temperature before serving.

mexican chocolate cake with chocolate-cinnamon buttercream frosting

This is my favorite chocolate cake. I make it for myself every year for my birthday and for all of my friends' birthdays too. This year I placed it too close to the edge of the countertop and left the room. When I came back there were lots of little fingerprints in the frosting! I think I know what I'll be making Daphne for her birthday next year.

naptime stopwatch

15 minutes prep time
45 minutes bake time

makes 1 bundt cake

cake

Unsalted butter, as needed

¾ cup unsweetened cocoa powder, plus more as needed

2 cups granulated sugar

1¾ cups all-purpose flour

1 teaspoon kosher salt

½ teaspoon chili powder

1 teaspoon ground cinnamon

1 teaspoon baking powder

1 teaspoon baking soda

1 cup cultured buttermilk

½ cup vegetable oil

2 large eggs

1 teaspoon vanilla extract

(continued)

1. Preheat the oven to 350°F. Butter a 9-inch Bundt pan and dust the inside lightly with cocoa powder. Set aside.

2. *To make the cake:* Sift the cocoa powder into a large bowl. Add the sugar, flour, salt, chili powder, cinnamon, baking powder, and baking soda and combine the ingredients with a whisk.

3. In an electric mixer fitted with the paddle attachment, beat together the buttermilk, vegetable oil, eggs, and vanilla on medium speed. Reduce the speed to low and add the dry ingredients slowly, stopping once to scrape down the sides of the bowl with a rubber spatula.

4. Pour the batter into the prepared pan and bake for about 40 to 45 minutes, or until a cake tester inserted at the cake's deepest point comes out clean. Allow the cake to cool in the pan for 15 minutes, then turn it out onto a wire rack and cool completely before frosting.

5. *To make the frosting:* In an electric mixer fitted with a paddle attachment, cream the confectioners' sugar and butter until completely smooth, about 2 minutes. In a small bowl, whisk together the milk, vanilla, cocoa powder, and cinnamon until a paste forms. Add this to the butter mixture and beat everything on medium to high speed until the frosting is light and fluffy, about 2 minutes. Scrape down the sides of the bowl as needed.

6. Frost the cake by dipping an offset spatula in warm water, wiping it dry, and then immediately spreading the frosting onto the cooled cake, covering the top and sides completely.

make-ahead tips: This cake can be baked up to a day ahead of serving it. To keep it fresh, wrap it tightly in plastic wrap once it has cooled and place it in the refrigerator. Bring it to room temperature before frosting and serving. The frosting can be made up to a day ahead as well. To store it, place it in a mixing bowl and press a piece of plastic wrap directly onto the surface of the frosting and keep refrigerated. Bring to room temperature before spreading it on the cake.

serving ideas: This cake fits just about any celebration. I think it is particularly fun to top the cake with mini-sparklers or red sanding sugar to indicate the heat and flavor.

frosting

3 cups confectioners' sugar

1 cup (2 sticks) unsalted butter, at room temperature

3 tablespoons whole milk

1 tablespoon vanilla extract

⅓ cup unsweetened cocoa powder

1 teaspoon ground cinnamon

eggnog cheesecake with cranberry glaze

This is a classic cheesecake with a festive twist. The addition of rum, cognac, and spices gives it a subtle eggnog flavor while the cranberry glaze creates the "wow" factor. The whipped cream cheese gives the cake a surprisingly light texture that is the perfect cap to a holiday meal.

naptime stopwatch

20 minutes prep time
1 hour 5 minutes bake time

makes one 9-inch cheesecake

cheesecake

32 ounces (four 8-ounce containers) whipped cream cheese, at room temperature

4 ounces (1 stick) unsalted butter, at room temperature, plus more as needed for the pan

1 (16-ounce) carton full-fat sour cream

1 ¼ cups granulated sugar

3 tablespoons dark rum

2 tablespoons cognac

2 tablespoons cornstarch

1 teaspoon vanilla extract

1 teaspoon ground nutmeg

5 large eggs

glaze

½ cup granulated sugar

½ cup water or cranberry juice

1 tablespoon cornstarch

¾ cup fresh or frozen cranberries, thawed

1. Preheat the oven to 400°F. Prepare a 9-inch springform pan by greasing it with butter on the bottom and up the sides, or spraying it evenly with nonstick baking spray.

2. *To make the cheesecake:* In an electric mixer fitted with a paddle attachment, cream the cream cheese, butter, and sour cream on medium speed until completely smooth, scraping down sides as needed. Next, add the sugar, rum, cognac, cornstarch, vanilla, and nutmeg. Beat on high speed until the mixture is creamy and well blended. Reduce the mixer speed to low and beat in the eggs one at a time, making sure the mixture is very smooth after each egg is added. The finished batter should be smooth and glossy with no visible lumps.

3. Carefully wrap the outside of the springform pan very tightly with aluminum foil so that it can be placed in a water bath. (You are not going for looks here. Wrap the aluminum foil as tightly as possible underneath and up the sides of the pan with at least 2 layers; you don't want the batter ruined by water seeping in!) Place the foil-wrapped pan on the bottom of a larger roasting pan or deep baking dish and pour the cheesecake batter into the pan. Reduce the oven heat to 375°F. Set the roasting pan in the oven, then pour enough warm water into the roasting pan to reach at least halfway up the sides of the springform pan. Bake the cheesecake for 65 to 70 minutes, or until it is set throughout the middle and the top is light golden brown. Turn off the oven and allow the cake to cool for an hour in the hot water bath with the oven door propped open with the handle of a wooden spoon. Remove the cooled cheesecake from the oven, cover with aluminum foil, and refrigerate for at least 4 hours before serving.

4. *To make the glaze:* Add sugar, liquid, cornstarch, and cranberries to a small saucepan. Simmer until the liquid is reduced by half and starts to get syrupy, about 7 to 10 minutes. Allow the glaze to cool to room temperature before drizzling over the cooled cheesecake to serve.

make-ahead tips: This cheesecake requires advance preparation so that the cheese will set properly. It will last for up to a week in the refrigerator in the springform pan covered with plastic wrap.

serving ideas: This is a towering cheesecake that is best served in thick slices, like the ones you see at a diner.

variation ideas: This makes an excellent plain cheesecake as well. For the plain version, omit the rum, cognac, and nutmeg and add 1 tablespoon of freshly squeezed lemon juice with the cornstarch.

plum cake

This is my friend Jen's great-grandmother Rose's famous sweet and fruity cake. It can be made with almost any kind of fresh fruit, making it the perfect recipe for nearly all seasons. When Jen first shared it with me I used a combination of blueberries and apricots since they were readily available. In the fall, I make it with plums, my favorite.

naptime stopwatch

15 minutes prep time
1 hour bake time

makes one 9-inch cake

6 ounces (1 ½ sticks) unsalted butter, at room temperature, divided, plus more as needed for the pie plate

½ cup granulated sugar

¼ teaspoon kosher salt

1 teaspoon white vinegar

1 large egg

1 cup plus 1 tablespoon all-purpose flour

1 ½ teaspoons baking powder

3 plums, pitted and sliced into ¼-inch thick slices (about 1 ½ cups)

½ cup packed light brown sugar

1 teaspoon ground cinnamon

Juice of 1 medium lemon

1. Preheat the oven to 375°F. Butter a 9-inch pie plate and set aside.

2. In a food processor fitted with a blade, pulse 4 ounces (1 stick) of butter and the granulated sugar until well blended. Add the salt, vinegar, and egg and process again until blended. Add the flour and baking powder and process until a dough forms and the flour is completely incorporated.

3. Scrape the dough into the prepared pie plate and press it into a smooth layer to come about halfway up the sides. The dough will be very sticky.

4. Arrange the fruit in a circle on top of the dough. If you are using two types of fruit, alternate slices and make a decorative pattern.

5. Dice the remaining 2 ounces (½ stick) of butter and place the dots evenly on top of the fruit. Sprinkle the fruit evenly with brown sugar and cinnamon and drizzle the lemon juice on top.

6. Bake the cake for 1 hour or just until the bottom crust is browned and a cake tester inserted comes out clean. Place the dish on a wire rack and allow it to cool to room temperature. Slice and serve with a scoop of ice cream or dollop of whipped cream.

make-ahead tips: This cake will stay fresh wrapped tightly in plastic wrap for up to a day before serving.

variation ideas: Jen told me she has made this with up to 3 kinds of fruit in one cake, her favorite combination being pluots, peaches, and blueberries. As long as the amount of fruit totals 1½ cups you can experiment with almost any kind of fruit combination you can dream up.

homemade raspberry ice cream

I love to make ice cream during the summer, but sometimes it's a pain to make the custard and trot out all of the equipment involved. This simple mix-and-freeze recipe only requires five ingredients, plus a bowl and a freezer. It's so easy it's a shame not to try it!

naptime stopwatch

10 minutes prep time

makes approximately 6 cups

3 cups (20 ounces) fresh or frozen raspberries, thawed if frozen

2 cups granulated sugar

1 teaspoon vanilla extract

1 teaspoon crème de cassis liqueur

2 cups full-fat sour cream, stirred well

2 cups heavy whipping cream

1. Combine the raspberries, sugar, vanilla extract, and cassis in a food processor fitted with a blade and pulse a few times until the raspberries are crushed and juicy. Pour the mixture into a large mixing bowl and fold in the sour cream and heavy cream.

2. Cover the mixing bowl with plastic wrap and place it in the freezer. Stir the mixture every hour until it has frozen, about 6 hours. Alternatively, chill the mixture in the refrigerator for 3 to 4 hours, then freeze it in an ice cream maker according to manufacturer's instructions. Scoop and serve!

make-ahead tips: The freezing process takes about 5 to 6 hours. Put the raspberry mixture in the freezer to harden in early afternoon, stir it a few times throughout the afternoon, and you'll have the perfect frozen dessert ready by dinner.

variation ideas: Strawberries, blueberries, chopped peeled peaches, and apricots are all excellent substitutes for raspberries. To add an extra hit of favor add in one or two teaspoons of fruity cassis.

watermelon-lime ice pops

These frozen treats are perfect for adults and children. Everyone will find the icy fruit flavor totally refreshing on a hot summer's day.

 naptime stopwatch

15 minutes prep time
6 hours freezing time

makes 8 (2-ounce) ice pops

4 cups seedless watermelon, cubed (about 1 whole seedless watermelon)

¼ cup granulated sugar

⅓ cup freshly squeezed lime juice, from about 3 medium limes

1. Purée the fresh watermelon in a blender until completely liquefied and strain out the solids with a fine-mesh sieve, reserving the juice. You should have about 2 cups.

2. In a small saucepan over low heat, combine the sugar and ¾ cup water to make a simple syrup. Cook until the sugar has completely dissolved, then immediately remove the saucepan from the heat and allow the syrup to cool to room temperature.

3. Add the lime juice and simple syrup to the watermelon juice and stir to combine. Pour the mixture into frozen pop molds and freeze for at least 6 hours.

make-ahead tips: The simple syrup can be made up to a week ahead of time. In fact, it is worth having some in your refrigerator all summer long to sweeten iced teas and desserts. The freezing time needed for the pops will depend on the molds. With my basic plastic mold they freeze in about 5 to 6 hours.

variation ideas: Many fruits can be combined with simple syrup to make popsicles. I've followed this basic recipe using peaches, raspberries, and strawberries with lemon juice. Add in some strained Greek yogurt to make creamy ice pops! This recipe will double or triple easily for a party. If you don't have ice pop molds simply freeze the popsicles in small paper drinking cups with wooden popsicle sticks and peel off the paper cup before serving.

toasted brioche ice cream sandwiches with caramel sauce

Island Restaurant is one of my favorite restaurants in Manhattan. I eat there any chance I get and I always order this decadent ice cream treat for dessert. After my months of campaigning, chef Dino Partone agreed to share the recipe. Now I can make it at home and order it when I am there. It is the best of both worlds!

 naptime stopwatch

8 minutes cook time
10 minutes prep time

makes 2 sandwiches

caramel sauce

¾ cup granulated sugar

2 tablespoons light corn syrup

⅔ cup heavy cream

sandwiches

4 (1-inch-thick) slices of brioche

1 tablespoon unsalted butter, at room temperature

2 teaspoons granulated sugar

½ teaspoon ground cinnamon

1 cup good-quality vanilla ice cream, softened and divided

¼ cup confectioners' sugar

1. *To make the caramel sauce:* Bring the sugar, ½ cup water, and corn syrup to a boil over medium-high heat in a medium saucepan. Cook without stirring until the sugar begins to turn light brown, brushing down the sides of the pan with a wet pastry brush as needed, about 8 to 10 minutes. Then, immediately turn off the heat and remove the pan from the stove. Quickly and carefully pour in the cream, standing back and whisking continuously with a large whisk until it is completely incorporated into the caramel. Allow the sauce to cool while you make the sandwiches.

2. Preheat the oven to 350°F.

3. *To make the sandwiches:* Spread some of the butter onto both sides of each slice of bread. Mix the sugar and cinnamon together in a bowl and sprinkle it evenly on both sides of the bread slices. Place the slices on a baking sheet and bake for about 8 minutes, or until the tops of the bread are golden brown and toasted.

4. Remove the bread from the oven and allow it to cool for 5 minutes. Scoop about ½ cup of the ice cream onto 2 of the bread slices. Use a spatula or the back of a wooden spoon to spread it evenly on the bread in one smooth layer. Close each sandwich with a second piece of toasted bread.

5. Cut the sandwiches from corner to corner to make triangles. Set out two plates, drizzle them with even amounts of the warm caramel sauce, and place two sandwich halves on each plate. Dust the tops of the sandwiches evenly with the confectioners' sugar and serve.

make-ahead tips: The caramel sauce can be made well in advance. To warm it up before serving the sandwiches, heat it in the microwave on high for 30 seconds, or until it is hot to the touch.

irish cream
ice cream bars

This is the grown-up ice cream treat all adults love. The combination of booze and chocolate is always a hit. Make these during the day and serve them to the adults at summer barbecues; everyone will love them!

naptime
stopwatch

25 minutes prep time

makes 2 dozen squares

2 ½ cups chocolate wafer crumbs (about 40 wafers pulsed in the food processor)

4 tablespoons (½ stick) unsalted butter, melted

½ cup plus 1 tablespoon granulated sugar, divided

2 pints good-quality vanilla ice cream, softened

½ cup Irish cream liqueur (such as Bailey's)

1 cup (4 ounces) coarsely chopped semisweet chocolate

2 cups heavy whipping cream

Cocoa powder, for dusting

1. Preheat the oven to 350°F.

2. In a mixing bowl, combine the cookie crumbs, melted butter, and ½ cup sugar and stir together until the crumbs are evenly moistened and the sugar is well distributed. Press the mixture evenly into the bottom of a 13 x 9-inch baking dish and bake it for 10 minutes or until the cookies are toasted and the crust is firm. Remove from the oven and allow the crust to cool to room temperature before proceeding, about 20 minutes.

3. In large mixing bowl, gently stir together the softened ice cream and the Irish cream until smooth and creamy, about 1 minute of gently stirring. Stir in the chopped chocolate and set aside.

4. Using a whisk or electric mixer, whip the remaining 1 tablespoon of sugar with the heavy whipping cream until it holds stiff peaks, about 4 minutes. Scoop out 1 cup of the whipped cream and fold it into the ice cream mixture until evenly incorporated. Reserve the rest of the whipped cream in the mixing bowl for later. To store it, cover the bowl with plastic and keep it in the refrigerator until needed.

5. Pour the ice cream mixture onto the cooled crust using a rubber spatula, and cover it with plastic wrap and place it in the freezer to set for at least 6 hours, or up to overnight.

6. Before serving, spread the reserved whipped cream over the ice cream and dust the surface lightly with cocoa powder. Cut into 2-inch squares and serve.

beverages

the ultimate double-thick mocha frappé

When I was pregnant I craved these every single day. It was fine when I was eating for two, but after Daphne was born I had to wean myself off of them! I still make them once in a while for a special treat. Now that Daphne is old enough to eat ice cream, I often make two servings during naptime and give one to her when she wakes up.

naptime stopwatch

10 minutes prep time

makes 2 large servings

2 scoops good-quality coffee ice cream

2 scoops good-quality chocolate ice cream

½ cup 2% milk

½ cup chocolate syrup, divided (I like U-Bet)

Whipped cream for serving

1. Add both ice creams and the milk to a blender. Blend until the mixture is soupy, but not too thin.

2. Drizzle ¼ cup of the chocolate syrup around the inside of 2 chilled glasses. Do this by tilting the glass and pouring the syrup down one side then swirling the glass around so that the syrup coats all the sides of the glasses. Pour the ice cream mixture from the blender into the glasses. Top each frappé with some of the remaining chocolate syrup and a dollop of whipped cream and serve!

daphne's chocolate egg cream

This is Daphne's favorite drink in the whole world. Sometimes I serve it for dessert, or sometimes I have one waiting when she gets home from school.

naptime
stopwatch

2 minutes prep time

Pour the milk and chocolate syrup into a tall glass and whisk the ingredients together with a fork. Then pour the seltzer in and whisk everything together as the glass is filled up. Serve with a straw!

makes 1 serving

½ cup 2% milk

3 tablespoons chocolate syrup
(I like U-Bet)

¾ cup seltzer water

sparkling sangria cooler

My parents' friend Bill Galvani was famous for serving this festive punch at his Cinco de Mayo parties in Cooperstown. My mom liked it so much that she wrote down the recipe, and I dug it out of her collection years later. Bill recently told me that he can't recollect the actual origin of this recipe, but remembers it having quite an effect on people. I can vouch for that fact; it is always a hit with our friends. Plan on letting the flavors meld for at least an hour.

naptime stopwatch

5 minutes prep time

Mix all ingredients in a large pitcher except ginger ale, and refrigerate for at least 1 hour or up to 1 day. Just before serving, stir in the ginger ale and garnish with orange and lemon slices.

makes 5½ to 6 cups

1 bottle (750 milliliters) dry red wine, chilled

½ cup brandy

½ cup orange liqueur (Triple Sec or Cointreau)

Juice of 1 orange

Juice of 1 lemon

6 ounces frozen lemonade concentrate, thawed (about ⅔ cup)

¾ cup ginger ale, chilled

Lemon and orange slices for serving

serving ideas: This is a festive drink that calls for a fun atmosphere. Serve it up in wine glasses and garnish with big slices of fruit.

variation ideas: I do not usually use frozen juice concentrates, but in this case the frozen lemonade gives it just the right sweetness that nobody can quite place. You can make lemon simple syrup instead if you don't want to use the frozen concentrate but I warn you: It won't quite taste the same.

strawberry margaritas

It's important to have a few easy cocktail recipes that can be whipped up quickly. These margaritas are my standby for summer entertaining. I adapted them from my friend Char's recipe for watermelon margaritas; I had a glut of strawberries and decided to use them instead.

naptime stopwatch

20 minutes prep time

makes 4 servings

1 lime, cut into wedges

1 cup rock salt (optional)

2 cups fresh strawberries, hulled

1 cup tequila

½ cup freshly squeezed lime juice

½ cup orange liqueur (Triple Sec or Cointreau)

¼ cup confectioners' sugar

3 cups crushed ice

1. If you'd like to serve the margaritas in salted glasses, pour rock salt into a wide shallow bowl or saucer. Moisten the rims of the glasses with lime wedges, then turn them upside down in the salt to lightly coat. Invert, and set aside. Reserve the lime wedges.

2. Blend the strawberries, tequila, and lime juice in a blender. Add the orange liqueur, sugar, and ice and blend until all of the ingredients are incorporated, about 2 minutes.

3. The strawberry seeds will settle to the bottom of the blender after it is turned off. Pour the mixture into glasses, being careful not to pour in the seeds. Garnish with the lime wedges and serve.

variation ideas: Watermelon can be substituted in this recipe to make Watermelon Margaritas. Or make them with 1 cup of strawberries and 1 cup of watermelon to make Strawberry-Watermelon Margaritas.

mom's special white hot chocolate

When the days get shorter and the temperatures drop this is just the thing to warm you up. Indulge in a hot mug after the kids have gone to sleep; it will quickly become your favorite winter nightcap.

naptime stopwatch

10 minutes cook time

makes 4 servings

4 ounces white chocolate, coarsely chopped

⅔ cup Irish cream liqueur

3 cups 2% milk

Pinch freshly grated nutmeg

1. In a large saucepan over low heat, slowly melt the chopped chocolate. Once it is smooth, pour the Irish cream into the pan in a steady stream, whisking continuously to incorporate it into the chocolate. Next, pour the milk into the chocolate mixture, stirring well to blend. Warm until heated through.

2. Pour the hot liquid into mugs and garnish each mug with a pinch of freshly grated nutmeg. Drink hot!

make-ahead tips: If you make this hot chocolate ahead of time, store it covered in the refrigerator and reheat it in a saucepan on the stovetop prior to drinking.

serving ideas: A big dollop of vanilla whipped cream is always a welcome addition to hot chocolate!

variation ideas: Dark chocolate can be substituted if white chocolate is unavailable.

pantry staples

perfect pesto

Pesto is the ultimate staple. In the summer, when I can pick the basil fresh from my garden, I make one large batch every week. I keep half in the refrigerator for the week and freeze the other half for winter. Pesto freezes very well. By the end of summer I'll have accumulated a stockpile to last me through the cold months when it's hard to find fresh local herbs. It takes barely any work to double or triple this recipe if you want to make more. Sometimes I add slow-roasted tomatoes (page 68) to give the flavor a tasty twist (see the Variation Ideas, below). Use a good-quality olive oil here.

naptime
stopwatch

10 minutes prep time

makes about 3 cups

4 cups packed fresh basil leaves

4 large garlic cloves

1 cup (4 ounces) pine nuts

1 cup (4 ounces) freshly
grated Parmesan cheese

½ cup (2 ounces) freshly grated
Pecorino Romano cheese

1 ⅓ cups olive oil

1. Combine the basil and garlic in a food processor and process to a fine paste. Add the pine nuts and process again until the mixture is smooth. Finally, add the cheeses and process until a thick paste forms.

2. With the machine running, pour the olive oil into the food processor through the tube and process until the paste loosens up and the pesto becomes smooth and creamy. If the pesto seems too thick, pour in up to ¼ cup warm water to loosen it up to desired consistency.

make-ahead tips: Pesto will keep in the refrigerator for up to 10 days in a sealed container. Or, if you want to save it for later, fill a freezer bag or small plastic container with pesto for up to 6 months. If it's in a bag, roll and press tightly to remove as much air as possible. Thaw by letting it sit at room temperature for 1 to 2 hours, until it is a spreadable consistency.

serving ideas: Pesto is a delicious and healthful condiment that pairs well with almost anything. It makes a great sauce for Spinach and Ricotta Ravioli (page 103). Daphne has come to love pesto and we make her a pesto-tortellini bowl at least once a week. Pesto is also great served on roast salmon or over any kind of broiled white fish like halibut or cod.

variation ideas: For Slow-Roasted Tomato Pesto, add 4 to 5 roasted tomatoes (see page 68) with the grated cheese, and process until smooth.

chive parsley butter

I often make a double batch of this during naptime and use it all month long. It can be used for everything from spreading on toasted bread to stuffing into the middle of burger patties for a tasty surprise.

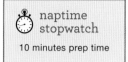

naptime stopwatch

10 minutes prep time

makes 8 ounces

1 cup (2 sticks) unsalted butter, at room temperature

2 tablespoons finely chopped fresh chives

2 tablespoons finely chopped fresh parsley

1. Cut the butter into large cubes and place it in a food processor fitted with a blade. Add the chopped herbs to the food processor. Pulse about 10 to 12 times, or until the butter is smooth and creamy and the herbs are completely incorporated. The butter should be a light shade of green.

2. Place a large square of plastic wrap on a clean surface and scrape the butter out of the work bowl onto the plastic wrap in one large mound. Fold up the plastic wrap firmly over the mound of butter and use your hands to shape the butter into a log that is about 1 to 1½ inches in diameter and 6 to 7 inches long. Twist the ends of the plastic wrap tightly so that no air can penetrate. The butter will keep in the refrigerator for up to 2 weeks, or can be wrapped in an outer layer of aluminum foil and frozen for up to 3 months.

variations ideas: Many different herbs can be used for this butter. Use whatever you have on hand to make up your own combinations. Basil, rosemary, oregano, mint, and sage are all excellent.

grandma's bread & butter pickles

My grandmother was an exemplary canner. By the end of the growing season in upstate New York her pantry was chock-full of all kinds of preserved fruits and vegetables in preparation for the cold winter. When she passed away, my father inherited both her recipes and her canning equipment. He took over canning for the family and has taught me how make all of our favorites. Of everything we make each year, these pickles are the standout success. We often distribute them around town at the holidays and neighbors knock on the door asking for a jar or two to serve at their summer picnics. We love to top Uncle Will's Killer Burgers (page 136) with a few slices of these pickles. Sometimes I just take a fork and eat them right out of the jar. This project is usually best spread out throughout the course of a day since the vegetables are salted and iced for 3 hours. If buying your cucumbers by volume, ask for half a peck or however many will fit in a 2-gallon container. The weight of half a peck will vary slightly depending on the water volume of the cucumbers.

naptime
stopwatch

1 day prep time

makes about 8 pints

8 pounds small cucumbers
(Kirby cucumbers are the best
for this)

6 medium yellow onions

3 green bell peppers

3 garlic cloves

1 cup kosher salt

Ice, as needed

5 cups granulated sugar

3 cups cider vinegar

2 tablespoons mustard seed

1½ teaspoons ground turmeric

1½ teaspoons celery seed

1. Sterilize 8 pint jars and 8 lids and rims and set aside (see Note, opposite page).

2. Wash the cucumbers well, cut them into ⅛-inch-thick round slices, preferably with a mandolin, and place them all in a very large bowl. Cut the onions, green peppers, and garlic into ⅛-inch-thick slices and combine them with the cucumbers in the bowl.

3. Pour the kosher salt into the large bowl with all of the vegetables and mix it well with clean hands. Be gentle with the vegetables so as not to break them. Pour the ice on top of the vegetable mixture and spread it in an even layer. Let the cucumbers rest, covered in ice, for at least 3 hours. The purpose of covering the vegetables with ice is to drain the cucumbers of excess water and help them get cool and crisp.

4. After 3 hours, pour the water and any remaining ice out of the bowl. Scoop the vegetable mixture into a colander in batches and rinse them under cold water until all of the visible salt is removed. Dry the vegetables on paper towels.

5. In a very large pot over medium heat, combine the sugar, vinegar, mustard seed, turmeric, and celery seed and stir until the sugar is dissolved and the brine is simmering. Add the vegetables to the pot and bring the mixture to a boil. It will take a while for the liquid to come to a boil, so be patient.

6. Once the mixture has reached a boil, turn off the heat. Ladle the vegetables and brine into the sterilized jars, leaving 1 inch of headspace

at the top. Wipe the rims of the jars dry with a clean kitchen towel and top each jar with the sterilized lids and rims. Only tighten the jar as much as you can twist with your fingertips; do not force it.

7. Bring a separate, very large pot of water to a boil. Make sure it is deep enough to cover the tops of the jars. Use a canning rack to hold the jars if you have one. If you don't, line the bottom of the pot with two layers of kitchen towels before adding the water so that the bottoms of the jars do not come directly into contact with the bottom of the pot.

8. Place the jars in the pot of boiling water. Bring the water back to a boil and process the jars in the water for 10 minutes, starting to time them after the water returns to a boil. Use a pair of long tongs and a silicone mitt to remove the jars and place them on a layer of dry kitchen towels on the counter where they will not be disturbed. Cover the jars with a second kitchen towel and let them rest for 24 hours. Through-out the day you'll hear the pop-pops of the seals on the jars forming. Resist the urge to pick them up; the seals will form throughout the day. After the jars have rested, check the seals by removing the rings and grasping the edges of the lid. If you can pick up the jar by holding the lid, the seals are good. Any jars that didn't fully seal should be stored in the refrigerator.

9. Store the jars of pickles in a cool, dry pantry until ready to eat. Refrigerate after opening.

make-ahead tips: I set aside 1 day a year to undertake this canning project. It is way too much to do this with Daphne in the kitchen, so I usually plan for her to spend the day with her grandmother or a babysitter. It is an efficient way to guarantee we'll enjoy our pickles all year long. It also is a nice way to plan my Christmas gifts early.

serving ideas: This recipe doubles and triples well. To give them as gifts, cover the lids with decorative circles of fabric, twist the rings on top, and tie them with pretty ribbons. They are terrific to give as hostess gifts, sell at bake sales, and use in gift baskets. As a child, I used to give them to my school teachers!

sterilizing jars, lids, and rims

The easiest way to sterilize canning jars is to run them through an empty dishwasher on high temperature without dish soap. Dry the jars in the dishwasher. If there are still droplets of water on the jars once they've been removed, invert them on a clean kitchen towel and allow them to air-dry. To sterilize rims and lids, drop them in a small pot of boiling water for 5 minutes. Remove with tongs and allow them to dry on a clean kitchen towel.

blueberry pie filling in a jar

I love fruit pies year-round; the only problem is that the fruits I love to bake with are the tastiest when bought locally and in season. I get around this by canning the fruit pie fillings when they are in season. This guarantees my pies will feature the flavors of summer, even in the dead of winter. I usually set aside 1 or 2 naptimes to can a few quarts of each pie flavor. With these jars in my pantry, it means I never have to buy flavorless imported fruit. These also make terrific holiday gifts. If you plan to give them away be sure to double or triple this recipe: Everyone will want one!

naptime stopwatch

1 hour cook time

makes 2 quarts

3 pounds (10 cups) fresh blueberries

1 ½ cups granulated sugar

6 tablespoons cornstarch

5 tablespoons bottled lemon juice

1. Sterilize 2 quart jars and 2 sets of lids and rims (see directions for sterilizing on page 207). Set aside.

2. Set a colander in the sink and add the blueberries. Rinse the berries with lukewarm water, picking out any debris or shriveled berries. Pour the clean berries onto a countertop lined with cotton kitchen towels and gently pat them dry so no visible drops of water remain.

3. In a large stockpot bring ½ cup water, sugar, cornstarch, and lemon juice to a boil over medium-high heat. Stir with a long wooden spoon until the sugar is completely dissolved.

4. Carefully pour in the blueberries and bring the mixture to a boil, for 5 minutes, or until the temperature reached 170°F, stirring continuously. Be sure to use a long spoon to protect your hands and arms; the mixture can bubble and spew as it heats up. Stir it at this temperature for about 5 minutes. The berries will release their juices and the mixture will thicken, becoming blue and glossy. Remove from the heat and set aside while you prepare the jars.

5. Set up the sterilized jars in the sink. Place a funnel over the opening of the first jar and ladle in the blueberry mixture, leaving about 1 inch of headspace at the top. Repeat with second jar.

6. Wipe the rims of the jars clean with kitchen towels. Place the sterilized lids on the jars and seal them with the rims, only tightening the ring as much as you can twist with your fingertips. Do not force it.

7. Bring a very large stock pot or canning pot of water to a boil. Make sure it is deep enough to cover the tops of the jars. Use a canning rack to hold the jars if you have one. If you don't, line the pot with two layers of kitchen towels before adding the water so that the bottoms of the jars do not come directly into contact with the bottom of the pot.

8. Place the jars into the water, and wait for it to return to a boil.

Process the jars in the water for 30 minutes, starting to time them after the water returns to a boil. Use a pair of long tongs and a silicone mitt to remove the jars and place them on a layer of dry kitchen towels on the counter where they will not be disturbed. Cover the jars with a second kitchen towel and let them rest for 24 hours. Throughout the day you'll hear the pop-pops of the seals of the jars forming. Resist the urge to pick them up; the seals will form throughout the day. After the jars have rested, check the seals by removing the rings and grasping the edges of the lid. If you can pick up the jar by holding the lid, the seals are good. Any jars that didn't fully seal should be stored in the refrigerator.

9. Store the jars of blueberry filling in a cool, dry pantry until ready to eat. Refrigerate after opening.

make-ahead tips: If you plan to double or triple your recipe, set aside more time to complete this project.

serving ideas: To make a perfect summery blueberry pie, use the pie crust recipe on page 156. Pop open one of these jars for the filling and bake it for 20 minutes, or until the pie is warm and bubbly. Serve hot and enjoy the taste of summer!

homemade marinara sauce

This sauce is a staple in my kitchen. On days when I have extra time because dinner is already prepared I make large batches of this to freeze. That way it is always on hand on days when there is no time to cook.

naptime
stopwatch

5 minutes prep time
50 minutes cook time

makes 6 cups

1 tablespoon olive oil

8 garlic cloves, thinly sliced

4 fresh basil leaves, torn

2 (28-ounce) cans crushed tomatoes, with juices

2 teaspoons kosher salt

2 teaspoons balsamic vinegar

1. In a large saucepan, warm the olive oil over low heat. Add the sliced garlic and sauté until they are lightly golden, about 3 minutes. Stir in the basil leaves.

2. Pour in the tomatoes and their juices, bring the sauce to a boil, and add the kosher salt. Then reduce the heat to low and simmer the sauce for about 45 to 50 minutes. As the sauce thickens up at the end, stir in the balsamic vinegar and remove the pan from the heat. Serve the sauce hot over pasta, or cool it to room temperature before storing.

make-ahead tips: This sauce can be stored in a sealed container in the refrigerator for up to 2 weeks. To freeze the marinara, fill a sealable container with the sauce and leave 1 inch of headspace at the top to allow for expansion. Fit the lid tightly on the container to prevent air from penetrating the container and freeze it for up to 3 months. Bring it to room temperature before warming on the stovetop after it has been frozen. This sauce can also be poured into glass jars and sealed in a hot water bath to be stored for longer amounts of time. For water bath instructions, see page 207.

Opposite page, from left: Grandma's Bread & Butter Pickles, page 206; Blueberry Pie Filling in a Jar, page 208

peppermint hot fudge sauce

After my mother-in-law made me the plain version of this decadent sauce, I never bought another jar of chocolate sauce again. It is incredibly easy to make and is so much better than anything found on store shelves. One year I added peppermint extract and gave out jars of sauce for holiday gifts. Everyone loved it so much that I received requests for it and it quickly became my signature holiday gift. Throughout the fall I set aside a few naptimes for making the hot fudge sauce. Then I seal the jars and store them in the cupboard until I give them out for Christmas.

naptime stopwatch

20 minutes cook time

makes approximately
5 cups or 5 half-pint jars

2 cups unsweetened cocoa powder

1 ½ cups granulated sugar

1 cup packed light brown sugar

¼ teaspoon kosher salt

2 cups heavy cream

1 cup (2 sticks) unsalted butter, cut into small pieces

2 teaspoons pure peppermint extract

1. In a double boiler or heatproof bowl placed over a pot of simmering water (do not allow the bowl to touch the water), stir together the cocoa, both sugars, and salt until the sugars begin to melt. Immediately add the cream and butter and stir everything together.

2. Cook this mixture over the simmering water, stirring constantly to make sure the sauce stays smooth. Scrape down the sides of the bowl and bring the mixture to a boil for 1 minute. The boil will look like a few heavy bubbles coming up from the bottom; it will not be a rolling boil. After you see thick bubbles for 1 minute, remove the sauce from the heat.

3. Allow the sauce to cool for 5 minutes, then stir in the peppermint extract with a wooden spoon.

4. Pour the sauce into a container with a lid and it will store well in the refrigerator for up to 3 months. If giving as gifts, pour the sauce into sterilized 8-ounce jars and process in a hot water bath for 10 minutes (see directions for sterilizing and processing on page 207).

make-ahead tips: The sauce will keep in a covered container in the refrigerator for up to 3 months (if it lasts that long!). A sealed sterilized jar will last for up to a year when stored in a cool, dry place. If made in big batches for gifts, the sauce can easily be placed in jars and sealed ahead of time. Store them in a cool dry place until you are ready to distribute them.

serving ideas: Warm this sauce in the microwave and drizzle it over just about anything for a treat. My favorite dessert is to fill an Everyday Cream Puff (page 178) with vanilla ice cream and drizzle it with this sauce.

variation ideas: For the plain version of this sauce, substitute 2 teaspoons of vanilla extract for the 2 teaspoons of mint extract.

strawberry-vanilla jam

Whenever we go strawberry-picking in the summer I come home and make this jam while Daphne naps. The jam-making method is so simple that anyone can do it. I usually double this recipe and seal half of the jars in a water bath so I can store them in my pantry until winter comes. There is nothing like sweet strawberry jam to brighten my mood in January! If I'm planning to use the jam quickly, I pour it into sterilized jars and store them in the fridge without processing in a water bath; it will stay in the fridge this way for up to 2 weeks.

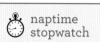

naptime
stopwatch

20 minutes prep time
40 minutes cook time

makes 3 cups or
6 half-pint jars

2 cups granulated sugar

Zest and juice of 2 lemons

2 pounds strawberries, washed, hulled, and halved

1 vanilla bean, halved lengthwise

1. Sterilize three 8-ounce canning jars and lids (see instructions on page 207) and set aside.

2. Combine the sugar, zest, and lemon juice in a large saucepan and warm it over medium heat. When the sugar begins to dissolve, add the strawberries and vanilla bean and allow the mixture to simmer for 30 to 40 minutes, or until thickened and glossy. To test if the jam is done, drop a teaspoonful on a chilled porcelain plate. If the drop of jam forms a skin and appears thick, then it is ready to be removed from the heat.

3. Allow the jam to cool completely before pouring it into containers. To process it in jars, remove the vanilla bean and ladle the jam into the sterilized jars. Close them with a sterilized lid and rim and place them in the refrigerator.

4. Alternatively, if you want to seal the jars in a hot water bath, process the jars in a hot water bath for 10 minutes. (See the directions for water bath canning on page 207).

chicken stock

Whenever we have a roast chicken I save the carcass to make chicken stock the next day. I set up the whole operation during naptime and let it simmer on the stove all afternoon. Then I freeze it all so it is always on hand for cooking.

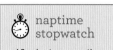
naptime stopwatch

10 minutes prep time
4 hours cook time

makes approximately
2 quarts

1 (3½- to 4-pound) roasted chicken carcass, meat removed

1 medium yellow onion, quartered

3 medium carrots, peeled and cut in half

2 celery stalks, ends trimmed and cut in half

1 head garlic, cut in half horizontally

10 sprigs fresh thyme

1 tablespoon kosher salt

1 tablespoon freshly ground black pepper

1. Combine all ingredients in an 8-quart stockpot. Pour in enough water so that the carcass is completely covered. Simmer everything uncovered for about 4 hours. Strain the mixture, reserving the stock and discarding the solids.

2. Pour the stock into containers, seal with lids, and chill for at least 24 hours in the refrigerator. Skim off the layer of fat from the top of the stock and repack the stock into containers and use immediately or freeze for up to 3 months.

vegetable stock

I never want vegetables to go to waste in our kitchen, so I make sure to use any kitchen scraps or leftover vegetables from recipes when making vegetable stock. This is essential in our kitchen, and I often set aside one naptime each month to make a triple batch and freeze it so that it is always on hand.

naptime stopwatch

20 minutes prep time
45 minutes cook time

makes approximately 4 quarts

2 tablespoons olive oil

1 medium yellow onion, peeled and chopped

1 medium carrot, peeled and cut into 1-inch pieces

1 medium celery rib, trimmed and cut into 1-inch pieces

1 medium leek (white and green parts only), trimmed, cleaned, and cut into 1-inch pieces

1 plum tomato, halved

4 garlic cloves, peeled and thinly sliced

4 quarts water

1 tablespoon kosher salt

1 bay leaf

2 sprigs fresh thyme

1. In a heavy stockpot, warm the olive oil over medium heat. Add the onion, carrot, celery, leek, tomato, and garlic and sauté for about 5 minutes, or until they begin to sweat.

2. Pour in 4 quarts water, salt, bay leaf, and thyme and bring the mixture to a low simmer for about 45 minutes. Strain the broth and discard the solids. Pour the stock into containers, seal with lids, and store in the refrigerator. Use within 4 days or place in the freezer and use within 3 months.

index

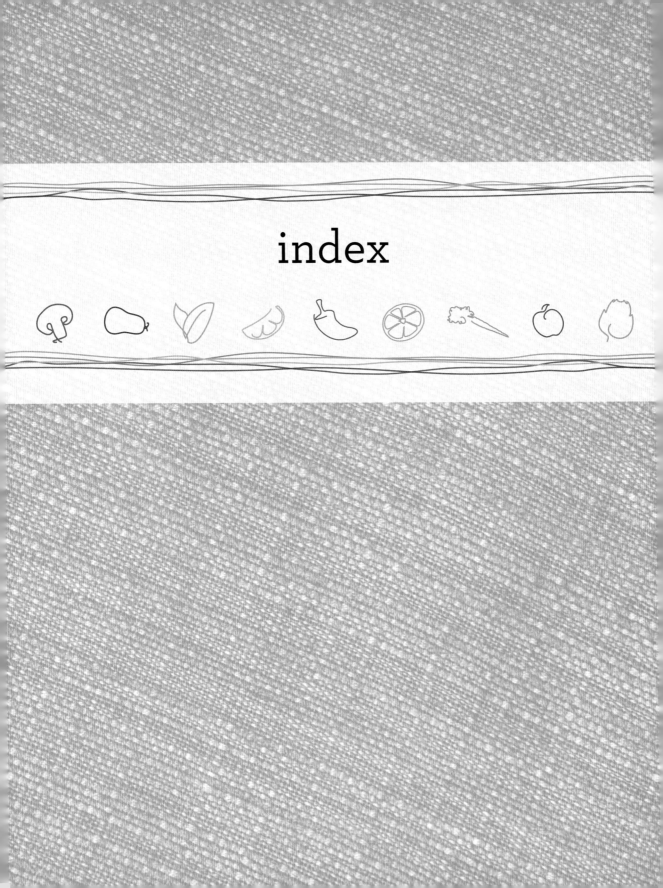

Note: Page references in *italics* indicate photographs.